Home Office Research Study 202

The parole system at work: a study of risk based decision-making

Roger Hood and Stephen Shute
with the assistance of Aidan Wilcox
University of Oxford Centre for Criminological Research

Research, Development and Statistics Directorate
Home Office

Home Office Research Studies

The Home Office Research Studies are reports on research undertaken by or on behalf of the Home Office. They cover the range of subjects for which the Home Secretary has responsibility. Titles in the series are listed at the back of this report (copies are available from the address on the back cover). Other publications produced by the Research, Development and Statistics Directorate include Research Findings, the Research Bulletin, Statistical Bulletins and Statistical Papers.

The Research, Development and Statistics Directorate

RDS is part of the Home Office. The Home Office's purpose is to build a safe, just and tolerant society in which the rights and responsibilities of individuals, families and communities are properly balanced and the protection and security of the public are maintained.

RDS is also a part of the Government Statistical Service (GSS). One of the GSS aims is to inform Parliament and the citizen about the state of the nation and provide a window on the work and performance of government, allowing the impact of government policies and actions to be assessed.

Therefore -

Research Development and Statistics Directorate exists to improve policy making, decision taking and practice in support of the Home Office purpose and aims, to provide the public and Parliament with information necessary for informed debate and to publish information for future use.

First published 2000
Application for reproduction should be made to the Information and Publications Group, Room 201, Home Office, 50 Queen Anne's Gate, London SW1H 9AT.

Foreword

This is a particularly timely report in view of the current review of parole announced by the Rt. Hon. Paul Boateng in the House of Commons on 11 February 2000.

Roger Hood and Stephen Shute have researched parole with great thoroughness. This is their third report – the first looked at parole before the implementation of the Criminal Justice Act 1991, the second looked at parole in transition and this third report completes the picture by assessing the impact of the changes introduced by the 1991 Act and subsequently.

I particularly welcome the way they set out the historical development of parole in relation to the recommendations of the Carlisle Committee on the Parole System, of which Professor Hood was a member. The Committee expected the use of parole to increase, instead it has declined. This report raises fundamental issues about how parole is now decided. It questions whether the current balance between public protection and reintegrating prisoners back into the community under supervision is correct. These are difficult issues but right at the heart of penal policy.

PAUL WILES
Director
Research, Development & Statistics Directorate

Acknowledgements

This study was commissioned by the Home Office Research, Development and Statistics Directorate (RDS) on behalf of the Adult Males Parole and Lifer Group (AMPLG, now known as the Sentence Management Group) of the Prison Service. We benefited greatly from the advice we received from Tom Ellis and Maureen Colledge at RDS and from the other members of the Advisory Group which was set up to support this research.

This study would not have been possible without the encouragement and active support we received from the Chairman, Baroness Prashar, and the then Chief Executive of the Parole Board, Mike Todd. Mike Todd mobilised the Secretariat of the Board to provide a remarkable service to support this work. We are grateful to all members of the Secretariat for the hard work they put in on our behalf, and especially to Rob Wilkinson, Pat Boshell, Lee Startup and Steve Powell.

We also received valuable advice and assistance from Nick Hearn and Adrian Scott of AMPLG, and from Mike Lock, Chris Kershaw and John Ditchfield of RDS.

We were ably assisted in this research by Carol Dowling, Jan Appleton and Aidan Wilcox who all made helpful comments when we were designing and testing the research instruments and who were responsible for carrying out nearly all the interviews of prisoners, Parole Board Interviewing Members (PBIMs), prison officers, probation officers and parole clerks at 14 prisons. This required great tact and skill, as did the observations of the interviews which PBIMs carried out with prisoners. The timetable within which this research had to be completed was very tight and we are extremely grateful to them for having stuck to their task with great tenacity. The other part of the fieldwork – observations of Parole Board panels – was carried out entirely by Roger Hood and Stephen Shute.

A large amount of data were generated by the fieldwork and we are also indebted to our research assistants, who were aided by Dr John Kelemenis, for entering it for computer analysis so speedily. Aidan Wilcox, who remained with the project after the fieldwork in the prisons had been completed, played a major role in coding and entering data and in responding, with patience and good humour, to our many requests for statistical calculations. He learned computing at a remarkable rate under the expert guidance of Dr Andrew Roddam, statistical adviser to the Centre for Criminological Research.

This research could not have been carried out without the warm support and co-operation we received from the authorities at the prisons concerned, prison staff, probation officers, parole clerks and the prisoners who allowed us to observe their PBIM interview and so readily answered our questions.

We are most grateful for the forbearance of those members of the Parole Board who allowed us to observe their interviews with prisoners, to sit in and take notes of their panel discussions, and who willingly took on the extra burden of answering our questionnaires.

We owe a particular debt of gratitude to Nicole Smith, Head of the Sentence Enforcement Unit (formerly the Parole Unit), and to Mollie Weatheritt and colleagues at the Parole Board for the very helpful comments they made and questions they posed after having read the first draft of this study. These spurred us to analyse the data further and to try to clarify some misconceptions.

Stephen Shute thanks the University of Birmingham and the British Academy for the research leave he was able to take in 1998 when this work began. Roger Hood gratefully acknowledges the research support he has received from All Souls College and the University of Oxford Law Faculty.

Roger Hood and Stephen Shute
Oxford, March 2000

The authors

Professor Roger Hood, CBE, DCL, FBA is Director of the Oxford University Centre for Criminological Research and a Fellow of All Souls College.

Dr. Stephen Shute is Reader in Law at the University of Birmingham and an Associate of the Oxford Centre for Criminological Research

Aidan Wilcox is a Research Officer at the Oxford Centre for Criminological Research

Contents

Summary of the main findings

The aims

This research was commissioned in August 1998 by the Home Office Research, Development and Statistics Directorate (RDS) on behalf of the Adult Males Parole and Lifer Group (now known as the Sentence Management Group) with the support of the Parole Board. The main aim, set out in the tender specification, was to 'assess the effectiveness and efficiency of current procedures and to identify areas where developments, improvements or different approaches are needed'. The research included an examination of: how dossiers are compiled; how the Parole Board assesses applications in relation to the Secretary of State's directions; how panel decisions compare with risk assessment scores; reasons for refusal or granting parole; the influence of probation officers' recommendations; the conduct and perceptions of interviews carried out by Parole Board Interviewing Members (PBIMs), and an assessment of the value they added to parole decision-making.

Methods of research

The fieldwork was carried out in two linked phases:

- *Phase 1* involved observing 150 interviews carried out by PBIMs in 14 prisons; interviewing the prisoner and PBIM concerned; and interviewing probation officers, prison staff, parole clerks and 100 prisoners who had recently been refused parole.

- *Phase 2* involved observing panel discussions and decisions relating to these 150 prisoners and other cases panelled at the same time: altogether about 440 prisoners. Panel members were asked to complete risk assessment forms. They were also asked to complete a questionnaire on the quality of the dossier and the extent to which the PBIM report had had an impact on their decision.

Preparing for parole

In general, the arrangements for gathering reports for the prisoners' dossiers worked well, although some worrying delays, affecting one in five cases, occurred. The change to open reporting and disclosure of dossiers to prisoners was rarely said to have caused problems for report writers. The majority of prisoners going through the review process thought well of the interviews conducted with them by staff and considered their reports to be complete, accurate, fair and easy to understand. Nevertheless, there was a good deal of ignorance about the parole process, especially of the criteria laid down in the Secretary of State's directions. Not surprisingly, the prisoners who had been refused parole were less complimentary about parole procedures. Only half considered that they were fair.

Parole Board members were in general satisfied with the quality of reports on which they had to base their decisions. However, a third of the reports from the police and from psychiatrists evoked some dissatisfaction from at least one panel member, as did one-fifth of the reports from prison officers and from home probation officers.

How panels went about their business

The following findings stand out:

- In almost every case the lead member came prepared with a clear YES or NO opinion, occasionally preceded by the word 'iffy' and occasionally having drafted reasons for both granting or refusing parole.

- In nearly six out of ten cases the lead member took a 'bottom-line' approach.

- The approach taken by the lead member, whether bottom-line or 'full introduction', had no effect on the proportion paroled.

- In more than eight out of ten cases the lead member's decision was followed by the other two members with no voice of dissent, and in a further ten per cent it was confirmed after some dissent and discussion. In fact, in only eight per cent of cases was the final decision different from the opinion initially expressed by the lead member.

- In only five out of more than 400 observed cases did one dissenting panel member persuade the other two to change their minds, and always from a YES to a NO: never from NO to YES.

The parole rate

The proportion of prisoners released on parole in the sample of 438 cases was 34 per cent. When 'weighted' to take into account the offence composition of the sample, this parole rate was virtually the same as the national figure for 1998-99. National parole statistics show that of all eligible prisoners reviewed between 1992 and 1995 about 70 per cent were released on parole at some point of their sentence. Under the DCR system, the 'any time' parole rate has dropped by a third to around 48 per cent.

Reasons given for granting or refusing parole

The main findings were:

- In 84 per cent of cases refused parole the written reasons mentioned specific indicators of risk, such as the seriousness of the offence, a previous history of sexual or violent offending, previous failure to respond to supervision and/or breaches of bail or 'breaches of trust' while on temporary release from prison.

- In 96 per cent of refusals mention was made of failure to address offending behaviour, either generally or in relation to specific areas of concern, such as drugs, anger, alcohol or sex offending. And in a third of these cases the panel stressed that 'more work' should be done or 'work consolidated' in prison rather than under parole licence in the community.

- In 29 per cent of refusals an inadequate release plan was mentioned, but in only a handful of cases were poor employment prospects or unfavourable domestic circumstances mentioned.

- More than 80 per cent of the refused prisoners interviewed said that the reasons they had been given by the Board were 'unfair', and half said they found them 'hard to take'. A quarter said they had changed their behaviour in response to the reasons, but most in a negative, dismissive direction.

- When granting parole, having satisfactorily 'addressed offending behaviour' was mentioned in 98 per cent of reasons; a satisfactory release plan in 73 per cent; and prisoners' expressions of remorse and regret in a third.

- That the risk of reoffending would be 'further reduced by a period of supervision under parole licence' (or something to that effect) was given as a reason for granting parole in 30 per cent of cases.

- The average period of licence granted to the 147 paroled prisoners was 330 days. The shortest period anyone gained was 50 days and the longest 775 days. Eighty-seven per cent of those paroled had a condition attached to their licence whereas, before the introduction of the DCR scheme, conditions were attached in half as many cases. Indeed, 44 per cent of those paroled had three or more conditions attached to their licence.

- Almost every prisoner denied parole, with no further review, had an 'offending behaviour' condition attached to their NPD licence: six out of ten had three or more conditions. Of the refused prisoners interviewed, a third expressed hostility towards conditions attached to a NPD licence.

Risk of reconviction and the release decision

The statistically-based actuarial risk of reconviction prediction score (ROR) developed by the Home Office was used to gauge the relationship between risk and parole decisions. A calculation was made, from information in the dossier, of the ROR for a serious offence (one which would lead to imprisonment) during the parole period (i.e. 'during the period when the prisoner would otherwise be in prison') and over a period of two years. Calculations of the risk of committing *any* offence were made over the same two periods:

- There was a strong and statistically significant correlation between actuarial ROR for a serious offence while on parole (called RORS) and parole decisions so far as non-sex offenders were concerned. In other words, whether members of the Board realised it or not, their release decisions reflected in a systematic way statistical risk of reconviction. However, there was no such correlation for sex offenders.

- For non-sex offenders only eight per cent of prisoners with a RORS of 17 per cent or more were released, compared with 83 per cent of those with a RORS of 2 per cent or lower.

- Half of the non-sex offenders had a RORS of 7 per cent or less (an average risk of 3.7%). Forty per cent of this group was denied parole. Thus, as regards risk of reconviction, the Board acted with considerable caution in these cases.

- It was even more cautious as regards sex offenders. Only 22 per cent of sex offenders with a RORS of 7 per cent or less (average 3.2%) were paroled, not much higher than the 15 per cent paroled where the RORS was 8 per cent or higher.

Factors associated with the parole decision

There was strong evidence that the Board took into account factors relating to the directions given to it by the Secretary of State, but in different ways for non-sex and sex offenders:

- The prisoner's criminal history – number of previous convictions, previous convictions for a sexual or violent offence, previous custodial sentences and previous breaches of supervision or bail – was highly associated with the parole rate for those convicted of non-sex offences.

- Factors associated with a less serious criminal history (especially no previous convictions) were given far less weight for sex offenders. Their parole rate was low whatever their previous history.

- Having no prison adjudications was associated with a high parole rate for non-sex offenders but not for sex offenders.

- Both non-sex offenders and sex offenders who had completed all the offending behaviour courses mentioned in the seconded probation officer's report were much more often paroled than were those who had not completed the courses.

- Sex offenders who denied the offence were very rarely paroled, despite the fact that their average RORS was no higher than that of non-sex offender deniers, a much higher proportion of whom were granted parole.

Risk and sex offenders

The parole rate for sex offenders was analysed in relation to the 'Simple Actuarial Risk Classification Procedure for Assessing Long-term Risk of Sex Offenders' which has been developed by Dr David Thornton of the Prison Service. This prediction instrument takes into account a number of factors specifically associated with the probability of reconviction of sex offenders, as well as whether that probability has been reduced by completion of the sex offender treatment programme (SOTP).

According to the 'Thornton Scale', the probabilities of reconviction for a sexual or violent crime over a period of two years are:

- Level I: on completion of SOTP 1 per cent, without SOTP 2 per cent

- Level II: on completion of SOTP 9 per cent, without SOTP 15 per cent

- Level III: on completion of SOTP 22 per cent, without SOTP 36 per cent.

The author's analysis showed that:

- One-third of the sex offenders in the sample were in Level I. They posed a very low risk of being reconvicted of a violent or sexual offence over two years, and obviously an even lower risk during a shorter possible parole period. Nevertheless, the Board was cautious, releasing less than a third of them.

- Four out of ten were in Level II, for whom the risk of being convicted of a further sexual or violent offence over two years was between 9 per cent and 15 per cent. Nine out of ten of them were refused parole. Those released were all judged by the panel to have had the risk they posed reduced by successful completion of SOTP.

- Just over a quarter were in Level III, the highest risk. Five (20 per cent) were released, all of whom the panel judged to have successfully completed SOTP.

- Overall, the statistical risk of reconviction according to the Thornton scale was a less strong predictor of release than whether the prisoner had successfully completed SOTP. Of those who had done so, the proportion paroled was virtually the same whatever the Thornton risk category of the prisoner had been.

- Thus, what is regarded by many as a more appropriate risk prediction instrument for sex offenders than the 'general ROR' did not, by itself, explain the low rate of parole granted to sex offenders as a category.

'Clinical' compared with actuarial assessments of risk

Comparisons were made between the prisoner's actuarial risk of reconviction score (which had been derived from a large scale reconviction study) and the lead member's assessment of that prisoner's risk of reconviction. This showed that:

- Fifteen per cent of prisoners had an actuarial ROR of a serious offence during the parole period of 20 per cent or higher, yet lead members estimated six out of ten prisoners to have such a high risk. They similarly overestimated the risk of being convicted of any offence during the parole period.

- As regards sex offenders, 73 per cent of prisoners fell into Levels I and II of the sex offender predictor (equivalent to a ROR of less than 20 per cent over two years). Yet, lead members overestimated the risk in more than half these cases.

Parole and risk reduction: Parole Board members' views

Lead members were asked to estimate risk of reconviction for a serious offence if the prisoner were or were not to be granted parole. For more than eight out of ten prisoners they judged the risk to be the same. From this it can be inferred that most Parole Board members did not believe that the longer period of licence afforded by parole would significantly reduce the risk posed by the prisoner.

The influence of probation officers' reports

There was a strong correlation between the recommendations made by both prison and field probation officers and parole decisions:

- Where both officers recommended parole and the ROR of a serious offence on parole licence was between zero and 7 per cent (average 3.5%), the Board accepted the recommendations in 71 per cent of cases. Where the ROR was 8 per cent or higher, they accepted the recommendations in 30 per cent of cases.

- Of all prisoners refused parole, four out of ten had been recommended by both probation officers. This may explain why so many of the refused prisoners interviewed were disgruntled and disappointed with the system.

- If the Parole Board had not refused parole to *any* of the prisoners who had been recommended as suitable by both probation officers, the parole rate for the sample would have been not 33.6 per cent but 59.6 per cent, 77 per cent higher.

- If the Parole Board had released on parole *all* prisoners who had *both* a low actuarial risk of reconviction for a serious offence while on parole licence (an average ROR of less than four in 100) *and* a recommendation from both probation officers, the parole rate would have been 43.2 per cent.

- This is equivalent to a 29 per cent higher parole rate, or approximately 550 more prisoners released on parole in a year. The release of more of these low risk prisoners would, in fact, *reduce* the average rate of reconviction for all parolees. Of the 550 extra prisoners released on parole only about four per cent would be expected, while on parole licence, to be reconvicted of an offence serious enough to warrant imprisonment.

Predicting parole decisions

Through the use of logistic regression analysis a prediction model of parole decision-making was calculated:

- The statistical model, which selected seven variables, correctly predicted the decisions made by the Board in 85 per cent of cases: 84 per cent of YES decisions and 85.5 per cent of NO decisions.

- Probability scores, derived from the combination of weights assigned to these seven variables for each case, were grouped into five equal bands: ranging from 20 per cent or lower to a greater than 80 per cent probability of being paroled. This revealed that nearly half the prisoners (48%) had a relatively low probability of release (20% or less) and in fact only four per cent of them were released. In other words, virtually half the cases considered by the Board stood almost no chance of being paroled. At the other end of the scale, one in six (17%) had a very high probability of parole (greater than 80%), of whom 89 per cent were paroled.

- Taking these together, Parole Board decisions were, for 65 per cent of prisoners, correctly predicted by the model 94 per cent of the time.

● Multiple logistic regression was also used to develop a model specifically to predict release decisions for sex offenders. The best model, which selected only the home probation officer's recommendation, correctly predicted 87 per cent of parole decisions: 94 per cent of YES decisions and 85 per cent of NO decisions.

The role, use and value of the PBIM report

● Both PBIMs and prisoners had positive things to say about the interview. PBIMs felt that more than 80 per cent of the interviews had helped the prisoner to present his or her case and nearly all the prisoners had been co-operative and respectful. For their part, a similarly high proportion of prisoners said that the PBIM had been respectful, fair- minded, willing to listen and had asked the right questions.

● There were, however, several complaints, the main one being that the interview had been 'rushed'; a fact recognised by many PBIMs.

● PBIMs said that 90 per cent of the interviews they had conducted had yielded relevant new information, not available in the dossier, which would assist the panel in its assessment of risk. But few said that it would make 'a lot of difference' to the prisoner's chances of parole.

● The prisoners were more optimistic about the impact that the interview might have: 45 per cent thought that it had increased their chance of parole and only six per cent (compared with 22% of PBIMs) thought it had decreased their chance.

● PBIM reports were rarely referred to during panel discussions: in only ten per cent of the cases observed. Analysis of lead members' responses to the questionnaire attached to each dossier showed that:

  ○ only one in 12 of their pre-panel decisions had been *changed* by something they had read in the PBIM report

  ○ in 76 per cent the PBIM report *confirmed* their initial decision

  ○ in 16 per cent the PBIM report had *no influence* at all.

● In the few cases where it had been said that the PBIM report changed the lead member's initial decision, 60 per cent were from YES to NO.

Conclusions and implications for policy

The findings of this research, summarised above, clearly have implications for policy makers and for the Parole Board itself. The most important of these concerns the use made of parole in the light of the evidence about the risk posed by some prisoners who were denied it. In taking account of the Secretary of State's direction to give priority to risk, members appeared to overestimate the degree of risk posed by many prisoners, as indicated by the actuarially-calculated risk of reconviction score. The authors therefore recommend that an updated ROR score should be calculated and that Board members should be directed to give weight to it when making their decisions.

The predictability of parole decisions, combined with the high degree of concordance between the decisions reached by the members of Parole Board panels, inevitably raises questions about the necessity for a meeting to be held to discuss every case. Some suggestions for streamlining decision-making are offered.

The findings relating to the limited use made of Parole Board Members' interview reports in decision-making suggests that the role of interviewing members needs to be reconsidered. The authors suggest that the Carlisle Committee's recommendation for the appointment of parole counsellors in the prisons might be given further consideration.

Finally, it is pointed out that the implementation of the Discretionary Conditional Release system has not been accompanied by any reduction in the length of prison sentences. Rather, prison sentences have increased somewhat in length while at the same time the use of parole has declined considerably.

Chapter 1 The research in context

The changed structure of parole

The parole system established by the Criminal Justice Act 1967 had, by the mid-1980s, produced so many tensions, anomalies and procedural inadequacies that a thorough review was necessary. That review was carried out under the chairmanship of Lord Carlisle of Bucklow.[1] It provided a blueprint for reforms which were introduced, with some modifications, by the Criminal Justice Act 1991. The Act, which came into force on 1 October 1992, removed the Parole Board's discretionary power to recommend the release of prisoners serving sentences of less than four years. They were to be subject to a new system of Automatic Conditional Release (known as ACR) after serving half of their sentence.[2] Powers to release on parole (now called Discretionary Conditional Release – DCR) were to apply only to those sentenced to a determinate sentence of four years' imprisonment or longer.[3] Prisoners deemed by the Parole Board to be unsuitable for parole would, as before, be released at the two-thirds point of their sentence – their 'non-parole date' (NPD) – or at a later date if they had 'added days' for prison offences.

The Act also made four other important changes relating to eligibility for parole and the supervision of prisoners following their release. First, prisoners were no longer to be eligible for parole at one-third of their sentence. They now had to serve at least a half. One consequence of this was that whereas all prisoners serving four years or longer would formerly have received at least two parole reviews, under the DCR system the majority of prisoners would only get one review. This was because the 'parole window' had been narrowed: a prisoner would have to be serving at least six-and-a-half years in order to receive a second review, and at least 12-and-a-half years to receive more than two reviews. Secondly, under the old system, prisoners not granted parole, but released after serving two-thirds of their sentence, received no statutory supervision from the probation service, even though they were regarded as the most unsuitable candidates for release on grounds of the risk they posed. The 1991 Act sought to remedy this anomaly by ensuring that all prisoners, whether released on parole or at NPD, would be subject to supervision until the three-quarters point of the sentence had been reached.[4] Thus, the Board was no longer to be faced with the dilemma of whether to keep a high risk prisoner in custody for as long as possible or to release the prisoner earlier on parole as the only means of ensuring that he/she received

---

1 *The Parole System in England and Wales. Report of the Review Committee* (1988) Cm 532 (henceforth Carlisle (1998)).

2 Once released they are under supervision by the probation service until three-quarters of the sentence has been served. During the last quarter of the sentence they are liable to serve the unexpired portion of the sentence should they be reconvicted of another offence committed before the sentence expires. Prisoners serving less than 12 months are not subject to statutory supervision by the probation service, but are liable to serve the unexpired part of their sentence if reconvicted during this period. For both categories of prisoner, release at half-way will be delayed if the prisoner has to serve extra days for breaches of prison discipline. For a valuable study of the working of the ACR system, see M. Maguire, B. Peroud and P. Raynor (1996).

3 The Parole Board retained powers relating to the release of life sentenced prisoners.

4 Under section 44 of the Criminal Justice Act 1991, sex offenders may be required to remain on licence until the whole sentence has expired. Under the Crime Sentences Act 1996, section 20, sex offenders can have their licence period extended for up to ten years.

some supervision. The Parole Board was also required to exercise its discretion over what licence conditions should apply to each prisoner, whether released early on parole or automatically at the two-thirds point of the sentence. Thirdly, in order that the whole sentence should 'have meaning', prisoners were to remain 'at risk' of being required to serve the unexpired portion of their sentence should they be convicted of another offence before the sentence expired. Fourthly, the 1991 Act gave the Secretary of State discretionary powers to make rules with respect to the proceedings of the Board, including the number of members to decide cases. He 'may also give to the Board directions as to the matters to be taken into account by it in discharging any functions'.[5] The Board itself was given power to authorise members to interview prisoners and is under a duty to take reports of the interview into account.

There were, as a result, major changes in procedure:

- Every prisoner is now interviewed by a member of the Parole Board. The Interviewing Member prepares a report but neither makes a recommendation nor sits on the panel deciding the case.

- With rare exceptions, every prisoner has a right to see all the reports in the dossier prepared about him/her,[6] including the Parole Board Interviewing Member's report, and to make representations about any matters contained in the dossier and the report.

- Every prisoner has a right to receive reasons in writing for the decision taken by the Board.

- Authority was delegated to the Parole Board to make the final decision (rather than a recommendation to the Secretary of State) whether or not to grant parole for those sentenced to less than seven years. Since December 1998 this power has been extended to cases where the prisoner was given a sentence of less than 15 years.

The Secretary of State's directions and parole criteria

The Carlisle Committee, after discussing the criteria for parole, reached the conclusion that:

The parole decision will, thus, be based upon an evaluation of the risk to the public of the person committing a further serious offence at a time when he would otherwise be in prison, as against the benefit both to him and the public of his being released from prison back into the community under a degree of supervision which might assist his

---

5   Criminal Justice Act 1991, section 32(6).
6   There is no statutory entitlement for the prisoner to see the parole dossier but it is administrative policy only to withhold a report if it is judged to raise matters prejudicial to security and the safety of victims or others. In this study we came across no instances where a prisoner was refused access to a report in the dossier.

rehabilitation and thereby lessen the risk of his reoffending in the future ... The risk to be assessed is whether a further serious offence might be committed. It would clearly not be right to prolong a person's detention for several months or even years simply on the strength of a fear that he could commit the sort of offences which would merit a non-custodial sentence or at most a short prison sentence.[7]

This approach was reflected in section 32(6) of the 1991 Act, which required the Secretary of State when giving directions to the Board to have particular regard to:

(a)   the need to protect the public from serious harm from offenders

(b)   the desirability of preventing the commission by them of further offences and of securing their rehabilitation.

These statutory desiderata were first embodied in directions issued in 1992 'for the release and recall of determinate sentence prisoners'. Four years later a new version appeared which, according to Prisons' Minister, Ann Widdecombe, was designed 'to tighten and clarify the framework within which parole decisions are made'.[8] The 1996 directions laid down the following policy and criteria to be applied by the Board:

*In deciding whether or not to recommend release on licence, the Parole Board shall consider **primarily** the risk to the public of a further offence being committed at a time when the prisoner would otherwise be in prison and whether any such risk is acceptable. This must be balanced against the benefit, both to the public and the offender, of early release back into the community, under a degree of supervision, which might help rehabilitation and so lessen the risk of reoffending in the future. The Board shall take into account that safeguarding the public may often outweigh the benefits to the offender of early release.*

Before recommending early release on licence, the Parole Board shall consider whether:

(1)   *The safety of the public will be placed unacceptably at risk. In assessing such risk, the Board shall take into account:*

(a)   *the nature and circumstances of the original offence;*

(b)   *whether the prisoner has shown by his attitude and behaviour in custody that he is willing to address his offending behaviour by understanding its causes and consequences for the victims concerned, and has made positive efforts in doing so;*

---

7   Carlisle (1998), paras 321-322.
8   See Written Answers, HC Debates vol. 277, col. 308, 10th May 1996. She added: 'There is a more explicit statement about the need to protect the safety of the public being a paramount factor; it is made clear that previous post-release behaviour must be considered; and emphasis is placed on the need to take into account, in the case of a violent or sexual offender, any previous convictions for violence or for sexual offences'.

(c)   in the case of a violent or sexual offender, whether the prisoner has committed other offences of sex or violence, in which case the risk to the public of release on licence may be unacceptable;

(d)   that a risk of violent or sexual offending is more serious than a risk of other types of offending.

(2)   The longer period of supervision that parole would provide is likely to reduce the risk of further offences being committed.

(3)   The prisoner is likely to comply with the conditions of his licence.

(4)   The prisoner has failed to meet the requirements of licensed supervision, temporary release or bail on any previous occasion and, if so, whether this makes the risk of releasing him on licence unacceptable.

(5)   The resettlement plan will help secure the offender's rehabilitation.

(6)   The supervising officer has prepared a programme of supervision and has recommended specific licence conditions.

The Carlisle Committee had expressed the hope that its recommendations, based as they were on reaching a balance between the risk to the public and the rehabilitative benefits to be obtained from early release, would enable 'a higher proportion of long-term offenders to be judged suitable for release from prison at the half-way point of their sentence'.[9] Yet, as early as 1993, the Parole Board's *Annual Report* predicted that the new directions, presumably because they gave primacy to questions of risk, would 'eventually contribute to a lower paroling rate'.[10] There is no doubt that the revisions made to the directions in 1996 were intended to ensure that this occurred. While the Board was still instructed to *balance* risk against benefits, it was also for the first time instructed to 'take into account that safeguarding the public may often outweigh the benefits to the offender of early release' (our emphasis).

However, it should be recognised that although they give primacy to risk, the Secretary of State's directions do not specify what level of risk it is acceptable for the Parole Board to take, or how the 'balance' mentioned in the directions should be interpreted and applied in individual cases. In other words, the directions leave room for members of the Board to exercise their discretion.[11] Furthermore, they are not constrained by any performance indicators in relation to the annual parole rate.

---

9   Carlisle (1998), para. 280.
10   Parole Board (1994), para. 138.
11   It is interesting to note that paragraph 1(2) of the 1992 Directions ('each case should be considered on its individual merits, without discrimination on any grounds') was omitted from the 1996 Directions. However, the first objective set out in the Parole Board's Corporate Plan is: 'To deal with all cases in a consistent and equitable manner taking into account any Directions given by the Home Secretary'.

Aims of the inquiry

This research was commissioned in August 1998 by the Home Office Research, Development and Statistics Directorate on behalf of the Adult Males Parole and Lifer Group (now known as the Sentence Management Group) with the support of the Parole Board. The main aim of the research, set out in the tender specification, was to 'assess the effectiveness and efficiency of current procedures and to identify areas where developments, improvements or different approaches are needed'. More specifically, the researchers were asked to examine:

- How dossiers for applicants are compiled in preparation for panel meetings of the Parole Board, including the input of prison staff, probation officers and inmates, and how far the information contained in them was considered to be useful by Parole Board members.

- The conduct and perceptions of interviews carried by Parole Board members, including an assessment of their 'added value' to parole decision-making.

- How Parole Board panels assess applicants for release, including:

  ○ whether/how the Secretary of State's directions and guidance on release are being followed in decision-making

  ○ what information and what factors are taken into account in order to determine suitability for early release

  ○ whether the process for making decisions is consistent

  ○ how panel decisions compare with risk assessment scores

  ○ the types of reasons given for decisions

  ○ the timeliness at all stages of the procedure

  ○ the views of Parole Board members, prison staff, probation officers and inmates on the current arrangements

  ○ the disclosure of assessments and reasons for refusal to applicants for parole.

Thus, in carrying out the research, it was necessary to undertake, within the constraints of time and resources, as thorough an examination as possible of all aspects of the processing of cases for parole and of decisions made by the Parole Board. The authors were asked to draw upon the findings to suggest what 'developments, improvements or different approaches' might 'speed up the parole system without reducing the quality of assessment', and perhaps reduce costs.

The scope and methods of the research

In order to gain information on the preparation of parole documentation and views on the parole system, a sample of current parole applicants was identified in 14 prisons situated in nine prison regions.[12] The institutions were chosen according to two criteria: first, that they had a sufficient number of current applicants for parole; and, second, that they represented a range of security categories.[13] Each prison was visited in advance to obtain the consent of the prisoners, 98 per cent of whom agreed to take part in the study. Three weeks were spent at each prison. Over a period of four months, the researchers were able to:

- Observe 151 interviews carried out by 23 Parole Board Interviewing Members (known as PBIMs).

- Interview the 151 prisoners, who were asked about their knowledge and experience of the parole process and their reactions to the PBIM interview.

- Interview the PBIMs, who were asked both about their general experience of carrying out interviews with prisoners and their assessment of the specific interview observed. The PBIMs were also asked to estimate, both before and after the interview had taken place, the prisoner's risk of reconviction. A further 30 PBIMs responded to questions about their general experience via a mailed questionnaire.[14]

- Interview 63 seconded probation officers (known as SPOs) who had written reports on these prisoners. SPOs were asked about their general experience of preparing reports and about the assessments they had made of the prisoners concerned. They also completed a risk of reconviction assessment form for each prisoner.

- Interview 112 prison officers about the preparation of Prison Parole Assessments (known as PPAs).

- Interview 16 parole clerks who were asked about the process of preparing dossiers and what difficulties (if any) they encountered in so doing.

- Interview 103 prisoners who had recently been refused parole.

In addition, a questionnaire and a risk assessment form were mailed to 137 home probation officers (known as HPOs) who had written Parole Assessment Reports (known as

---

12 Central Area; Kent; London South; Mercia; Mersey and Manchester; North London and East Anglia; North West; South Coast; Yorkshire.

13 The following prisons were chosen. Category B: Swaleside and Maidstone; Category C: The Mount, Featherstone, Stafford, Littlehey, The Verne, Albany, Camp Hill, Wymott; Category C with Cat D sections: Downview, Lindholme and Wealstun; Category D: Sudbury. Because of the very small number of female parole applicants passing through the system at any one time it was not feasible to include a women's prison in the study. However, amongst the cases observed at the Board there were seven women. They were not excluded from the sample.

14 Two PBIMs did not respond to the questionnaire.

PARs) on the 151 prisoners whose interviews had been observed. Replies relating to 126 prisoners (83%) were received.

The second phase of the research involved observing Parole Board decision-making. The dossiers of the 151 prisoners seen in prison ('tracked prisoners') were allocated by the Parole Board Secretariat, usually seven or eight at a time, to a Parole Board panel where they were considered alongside other cases: 24 cases to a panel. The authors were present at 20 panels where they took as full notes as possible of the discussion. We had full access to the dossiers and were provided with copies of the reasons given for decisions. Many Board members made their notes available to facilitate the preparation of transcripts.

Thus, in this phase of the research:

- Decisions relating to 417 DCR cases were observed.[15] Information was also gathered on a further 21 DCR prisoners who had been interviewed in prison but whose dossiers were allocated in error to 16 panels that were not observed. Thus, information was available on 438 DCR cases.

- On our behalf, the Secretariat attached a questionnaire to each dossier sent to panel members. This – in relation to each case – sought their views on the quality of the reports in the dossier and on the value to them of the PBIM report. Attached to each dossier was the same risk of reconviction assessment form that PBIMs, SPOs and HPOs had been asked to complete. The form asked panel members to estimate the risk (from low to very high) of the prisoner being convicted of a serious offence (the kind for which imprisonment is the norm) over three time periods:

  ○ during the period of parole licence

  ○ over a period of two years if parole were granted

  ○ over a period of two years if parole were not granted.

Identical questions were asked about the probability of committing any offence over the same three periods. The form is reproduced as Appendix 4.

A comparative perspective

The authors have carried out two earlier studies of the parole system. The first dealt with the way the system operated before the introduction of the DCR scheme in 1992. Through interviews with 200 prisoners, 60 prison staff and 20 seconded probation officers in five

---

15   A further seven DCR cases were deferred to another panel, so the final decision could not be observed. A few other cases were withdrawn on the day and a few were being reconsidered after an earlier grant of parole because of a change in circumstances. These were excluded from our analysis of decision-making. Decisions on 14 'existing prisoners' were too few for detailed analysis. To avoid confusion, they have not been considered in the report.

prisons, and by observing 383 decisions made by Parole Board panels, it established a base-line of information about the 'old parole system' against which the changes in parole procedures and decision-making introduced by the 1991 Act could be assessed.[16] The second study was based on observations of 545 decisions made by the Parole Board in 1993 and 1994 in respect of 'existing prisoners' sentenced prior to 1 October 1992.[17] This phase of research was carried out in order to assess the impact of the 1992 directions on parole decision-making, albeit with respect to prisoners considered under the 'old system' who would receive no supervision unless released on parole. Both these studies have made it possible to make some comparisons between past practice and the use of parole under the policy and procedures currently laid down for Discretionary Conditional Release.

Plan of the report

Chapter 2 explains the timetable and procedures for preparing cases for parole review. It also discusses:

(i)   how parole clerks collated dossiers and the problems they encountered in obtaining information;

(ii)   what the prisoners knew about the system; what they thought about the interviews on which the reports about them were based; and what they thought of the dossiers that were disclosed to them;

(iii) how the various report writers viewed the system; how they gathered information for their reports and what training they were given; whether disclosure of their reports to the inmates affected what they wrote; and how valuable they thought their reports were to the Board;

(iv)   the extent to which Board members were satisfied with the reports contained in the dossiers they received and with the presentation of the dossier as a whole; and

(v)   how often prisoners' dossiers were not reviewed by a panel until after the prisoner's parole eligibility date (PED); and what the extra cost of these delays might be.

Chapter 3 considers the Board at work. It describes the composition of panels in relation to the statutory categories of membership of the Board, the approach taken by the person leading the discussion, known as the 'lead member', and the extent to which there was discussion of cases and disagreement between panel members. The reasons given for panel decisions are analysed in relation to the Secretary of State's directions. Particular

16   Hood and Shute 1994.
17   Hood and Shute (1995), also Hood and Shute (1996).

attention is paid to the weight given to completion of offending behaviour courses, to denial, remorse, release plans, and to the value of extended supervision as a means of further reducing risk. The number and type of conditions attached to parole and NPD licences are examined.

Chapter 4 examines the extent to which decisions to grant or deny parole reflect the statistically calculated risk of reconviction (ROR) for a *serious* offence, or for *any* offence, during the parole period – the only actuarially-based measure of risk of reconviction on parole at present available. The special case of sex offenders is considered separately. For these prisoners the relationship between the decisions made by the Parole Board and the risk prediction model devised by Dr David Thornton of the Prison Service was analysed. Called an 'Actuarial Procedure for Assessing Long-term Risk of Sex Offenders', the Thornton predictor takes into account whether or not the prisoner has completed a sex offender treatment programme (SOTP). Finally, the chapter concludes with a comparison between the ROR and 'clinical' assessments of risk made, for this study, by the panel members and probation officers.

Chapter 5 analyses the influence of (home and seconded) probation officers' recommendations on parole decisions and their relationship to ROR scores. In Chapter 6 it is shown (by using the statistical method of logistic regression) that a substantial proportion of the decisions made by the Board could be predicted on the basis of factual material available in the prisoners' dossiers. The chapter concludes by demonstrating the value of a statistical model of this kind for monitoring the Board's decisions – in this case by comparing the parole rates of prisoners from different ethnic backgrounds.

Chapter 7 analyses the role and value of Parole Board Interviewing Members' interviews and reports. It examines how PBIMs carried out and viewed their task; what prisoners thought of the PBIM interview compared with how PBIMs viewed it; and what impact the interview had on PBIMs' assessments of risk of reconviction compared with their assessments based on reading the dossier alone – in other words, what 'added value' they thought the interview had provided. The chapter ends with an analysis of the extent to which panel members believed that the PBIM report had changed, confirmed, or added nothing to the decision they would have made on the basis of other information in the dossier, had the PBIM report not been available to them.

Chapter 8 discusses some implications of the findings for parole procedures and paroling policy. The report concludes with four supporting Appendices.

Chapter 2   Preparing for parole

Producing the dossier

The current parole timetable starts 26 weeks in advance of the parole eligibility date – PED – or its anniversary in the case of second or subsequent reviews. Parole clerks in each prison are responsible for preparing the prisoner's dossier. They are required to obtain details about the offence from at least one of the following sources: the police, a pre-sentence probation report or a pre-sentence psychiatric report. In addition, the dossier must contain information on the prisoner's previous convictions (if any); remarks by the sentencing judge (if available); previous parole dossiers and reasons for refusal (if applicable); any adjudications and added days; reports on any courses undertaken in prison; and reports from psychologists and/or psychiatrists, if applicable. It must also include a Prison Parole Assessment from a prison officer and a report from a seconded probation officer. All these documents are disclosed to the prisoner, who may, if he or she wishes, make written representations to the Board. The dossier is then sent to the Parole Board Interviewing Member who arranges to see the prisoner between 15 and 16 weeks before his or her PED. After the interview, the PBIM prepares a report which is made available to the prisoner. Any written comments the prisoner may wish to make on it will be forwarded to the Board. By 13 weeks before PED, the home (field) probation officer, who will be responsible for supervising the prisoner on licence, should have submitted a Parole Assessment Report to the parole clerk, who must send a copy to the prisoner, who may in turn comment on it. The completed dossier is then forwarded to the Parole Board Secretariat. If the timetable is complied with, it should (at the time the fieldwork for this research was carried out) have reached the Board 11 weeks before the prisoner's PED.[17] This is to give sufficient time for the Secretariat to send copies of the dossier to three members of the Board, each of whom will review 24 dossiers before meeting as a panel in London to reach a joint decision. If there are no delays, the panel is convened seven weeks before the prisoner's PED or its anniversary.

It is the duty of the parole clerk in each prison to ensure that the complete dossier is sent to the Secretariat in good time. Clerks sometimes found this difficult to do. The problems most frequently encountered were obtaining reports from the police on the offence and/or the prisoner's previous record and the late arrival of reports from home probation officers. Concern was also expressed about prisoners being transferred into or out of their prison during the parole process. Nonetheless, it was rare for a dossier to be returned by the Secretariat to a parole clerk on the grounds that it had been inadequately prepared. Indeed, a check of the contents of the 438 dossiers considered at the panels revealed that the reports regarded as 'mandatory' were nearly always available.[18]

---

17   This timetable was subsequently changed. See page 19 below.
18   Police reports had been obtained for 77 per cent of dossiers, pre-sentence reports for 59 per cent and pre-sentence psychiatric reports for 11 per cent. In fact, 92 per cent of dossiers had at least one or other of these reports. In only one dossier was a home probation report missing, another dossier was missing a prison parole assessment, and in eight dossiers (1.8%) there was no report from the seconded probation officer, because it was not the policy in the prisons concerned to prepare one for all prisoners.

Apart from some minor suggestions for improvement,[19] all the parole clerks said that the instructions contained in the Prison Service's *Parole Release and Recall Manual* (PSO 6000) were very helpful. Most of them, however, found the computerised Inmate Information System – known as IIS, which was designed to co-ordinate information on the status of the prisoner's parole application, rather difficult to use, and half said that they would benefit from more support from their managers in the prison. Attempts have been made recently to iron out these difficulties.

Arranging the Parole Board member's interview

The majority of PBIMs said that, when they received the dossier prior to their interview with the prisoner, information about the offence was too often missing. Furthermore, observations at the prisons revealed that there was no systematic procedure for ensuring that course reports and mandatory drug testing reports were always included in the dossier sent to the PBIM. Although PBIMs recognised it was not current policy, many felt that it would be helpful to them if the dossier at this stage could have included the PAR from the home probation officer. This was probably because the Board's guidance note for PBIM interviews (para 10.21) states that the PBIM is required to 'confirm any plans in the PAR and check their viability' although the note goes on to say that, if the interview is conducted on time, no PAR may be available and therefore 'more questions will need to be asked'. It is not surprising that a PBIM asked to assess the resettlement plan of a prisoner would rather have the home probation officer's report than rely on what the prisoner has to say. Clearly the Board has a dilemma here. If the PAR were to be made available to the PBIM before the interview, there would be a danger that the home circumstances could have changed drastically by the time a panel considered the case some two months later.

Another recurrent theme voiced by PBIMs was the trouble they had in arranging interviews at some prisons and the constraints placed on them by the prison timetable. A few PBIMs said that sometimes officers were not expecting them or there had been a lack of communication between the parole clerk and staff manning the prison gate or on a wing. Typical comments were:

Many prisons don't put themselves out to facilitate parole interviews. They think parole should fit around the normal regime.

Prisons don't take parole very seriously.

Prisoners not being in prison when I come to do the interview; wing landing staff claiming not to know that interviewing was to take place.

Trying to fit in with prison officers' meal times.

---

19   Parole clerks said there would be a considerable saving in staff time and photocopying costs if PBIMs returned their copy of the dossier to the parole clerk when submitting the report of their interview with the prisoner.

Although a 'liaison PBIM' is appointed to each prison to ensure the smooth working of the system, it would seem that more needs to be done in some prisons to ensure that prison staff are made aware by management of their duty to facilitate efficient use of Parole Board members' time.

Concern was also expressed that too many prisoners received dossiers too late to be able to digest them properly in time for the interview. PBIMs said that often the purpose of the interview had not been explained to the prisoner in advance. No one, including their personal officer, had helped them understand their dossier. This must put such prisoners at a disadvantage. Perhaps some reconsideration should be given to the recommendation of the Carlisle Committee that a cadre of trained volunteer 'parole counsellors' should be established at each prison to help prisoners who would 'find it hard to make anything of the dossier, still less compose written representations of their own without help'.[20]

Collecting information for reports on the prisoner

Report writers were asked how they collected the information on which they based their reports. Prison staff and probation officers said that they relied not only on their interview with the prisoner but also on prison and probation records. They often shared information: seconded and home probation officers said they liaised on at least 80 per cent of prisoners before writing their individual reports. It is not surprising therefore that for more than 80 per cent of prisoners they concurred in their recommendation (see Table 5.1, page 52 below).

Those who prepared reports were also asked whether they were given enough time for the job. Only a minority of seconded probation officers (16%) said that they were not, even though most said that a parole report took them the best part of a working day to prepare. However, half of the home probation officers said that they sometimes found it difficult to submit their report to the prison on time. In addition to the pressures created by other work, 30 per cent of these officers complained that the deadline was too short, and a fifth mentioned the time and expense entailed in travelling to prisons to interview prisoners. A third of the prison officers complained that no time was allocated specifically for the preparation of the PPA report. They were also rather sceptical of the use made by the Board of their reports: only a quarter (27%) thought that the Board took 'a lot of notice' of them and half said they sometimes disagreed with the reasons given by the Board for refusing parole.

Disclosure of reports to inmates had been recommended by the Carlisle Committee.[21] In our base-line study in 1992, the majority of the prison and probation officers who were interviewed were, in principle, in favour of inmates seeing their reports. Nevertheless, about half had been concerned lest this should make reports more circumspect and therefore 'weaker'. A third of the prison officers and half the probation officers were also worried that open reporting might cause disciplinary problems.[22] In this study it was found that these

---

20   See also page 75 below.
21   Carlisle (1988), paras 337-341.
22   Hood and Shute (1994), paras 99-105.

fears have largely proved to be groundless. Only 10 per cent of prison officers could recall ever having been inhibited by disclosure of their report to an inmate. When asked specifically about the reports they had written on the 'tracked' prisoners, seconded probation officers said that they had been inhibited in what they wrote about the inmate in only five per cent of the cases. But home probation officers told us that such inhibitions had affected 15 per cent of the reports they had written. It was not surprising that this proportion was higher than for SPOs, given that the HPOs would have to supervise the prisoner whether released on parole or at NPD:

I have to remember that whatever the result of the Board I have to maintain a reasonable working relationship with the offender.

To say categorically 'No Parole' in a report on a dangerous man does cause potential dangers to the author who may be liable to threats when that man is released.

Very few of the report writers said that they had received any training specifically related to the task of preparing a report for the Parole Board:

- Only 15 per cent of prison officers reported that they had been trained for this task. Furthermore, three-quarters said that they had never received feedback of any kind on the quality of their work, and 95 per cent said that they had never been asked by the governor countersigning their report to change anything in it. This is probably why two-thirds of officers said they would like more support in carrying out this task.

- Only one in ten seconded probation officers said they had received specific training in writing reports for parole reviews.

- Rather more of the home probation officers (one-quarter) said they had received training specifically relating to parole. But, of those who had been trained, nearly half said it had occurred more than five years ago, before the new DCR system had got into its stride. Thus, half of the officers said they felt they needed more training, the majority mentioning risk assessment or a better understanding of what information the Parole Board required.

These findings may explain why some Parole Board members (see pages 17-18 below) were critical of some of the reports they received, especially as regards risk assessment. This might be overcome if the Board were more frequently to inform the report writer when a report is regarded as inadequate for its purposes.[23] More generally, the Board might consider whether it should give specific guidance to each category of report writer on the kind of information it requires.

---

23   At present the Board does occasionally draw the probation services' attention to inadequate reports from home probation officers when the panel has registered a complaint but not, as yet, to complaints made about seconded probation officers' reports.

The prisoners' perspective

The 151 prisoners whose dossiers were in the process of being prepared (90% of whom were having their first review), as well as the 103 who had recently been refused parole, were asked about their knowledge of the system. In general it was quite poor. Very few of either group said they had seen the Secretary of State's directions setting out the criteria for parole, and about 90 per cent said they had no idea how to obtain a copy. Knowledge of how the Parole Board processed cases at panels, the size of panels, and what sorts of people sat on them was also limited. For example, only 10 per cent of the prisoners spontaneously mentioned that probation officers sat on the Board and when asked directly whether they did, little more than a half said yes. This figure is much the same as that found in the base-line study in 1992, despite the fact that the system is now intended to be more open and prisoners do meet a member of the Parole Board. Recognising that parole applicants need to be better informed, the Prison Service is arranging for a booklet explaining the procedures and the criteria to be distributed to long-term prisoners. Perhaps consideration could also be given to making a realistic video.[24]

On the positive side, at least three-quarters of the tracked inmates thought that their interviews with prison and probation officers had been conducted carefully and that enough time had been allocated to them. This compares quite favourably with the views of prisoners processed under the 'old system' in 1991/92. At that time only about 50 per cent of the prisoners thought the interviews with prison and probation officers had been 'very carefully or carefully' carried out. Even though about a third of both tracked and refused prisoners in 1998/99 said that the person who had written the report about them had not known them at all,[25] 54 per cent rated the interview and subsequent report positively in terms of length, accuracy, fairness and completeness. In 1991/92, under the old system, only a third rated their interviews positively in these terms, and of course they had been given no sight of the reports in their dossier. Despite the more positive views engendered by the new DCR system, about one in five prisoners complained to the PBIM about some aspect of their dossier. The following exchanges occurred at PBIM interviews:

Case 33: [serving four years five months for burglary]

PBIM: *Your personal officer says you struggle to get on with staff. Do you agree?* Inmate: *No. I don't know why it was said. I had an interview with my personal officer lasting ten to fifteen minutes.* PBIM: *So he didn't know you?* Inmate: *No.*

---

24   In an internal report to the Adult Males, Parole and Lifer Group of the Prison Service, Mike Shepherd noted that the Prisoners Information Book (published in 1996) gave some useful information. Nevertheless, he pointed out: "It is doubtful that this helps a prisoner arrive at a realistic understanding of what to expect from the parole system prior to submitting an application'. See M. Shepherd (1998), p. 15.

25   This was broadly confirmed by the report writers themselves. For example, home probation officers said that they had felt they knew less than one in five of the prisoners 'very well'. The situation as regards the prisoners has not changed dramatically since 1992, when only four out of ten prisoners interviewed said that they had known the seconded probation officer who had interviewed them 'very well' or 'quite well', and half said the same thing about the prison officer. See Hood and Shute (1994), p. 16, fn. 31.

Case 81: [serving six years six months for arson and burglary]

PBIM: *Your prison probation officer says it's difficult to assess your risk and is unable to recommend parole. What's your attitude?* Inmate: *At the end of the day she don't know me. I only seen her twice – 10 minutes maximum.*

Case 142: [serving four years six months for robbery]

Inmate: *I only met my home probation officer once. She don't know nothing about me to write a report. She seems OK but she doesn't know me. She wrote a load of rubbish.* PBIM: *What rubbish?* Inmate: *She said my mum's address wasn't suitable for parole. It's the best place.* PBIM: *Why?* Inmate: *I asked her and she didn't answer me ... How can people judge just by looking at the records?*

It is hardly surprising that those who had been recently refused parole were more often critical of the system as a whole. Indeed, while two-thirds of the tracked prisoners said that they thought that, overall, the parole procedures were fair, this opinion was held by only half of those who had been refused parole. Furthermore, three-quarters of those refused thought that in general the outcome of parole applications was unfair: by which they meant that not all those who deserved parole got it and not all those who got it deserved it.

After they had been interviewed and seen their dossiers, prisoners were asked what they thought their chances of parole were. Only one in ten rated their chance of getting it as 'very high' and a further 17 per cent as 'high'. At the other end of the scale 40 per cent thought it to be 'low' or 'very low'. They proved to be realists, for 60 per cent of those who thought their chances to be high or very high were in fact paroled, compared with only two of the 60 prisoners who rated their chances as low or very low. And of those who had rated their chances as '50/50', exactly 50 per cent were granted parole.

One of the things prisoners mentioned to make the system more fair was that some restriction should be placed on how much weight the Board should give to their previous criminal history, particularly things that they regarded as 'water under the bridge'. This is an area where there is bound to be some conflict between prisoners' expectations and the Board's task as defined by the Secretary of State's directions. Prisoners consider that parole should be granted if they produce evidence (especially when endorsed by probation officers) that they have 'changed' during the course of their sentence. There is, after all, nothing else that they can do to counter the risk as indicated by their past behaviour.

However, the 1996 directions make it clear that the Board must take into account both the nature and circumstances of the original offence and any past failures to meet the requirements of supervision, temporary release or bail, and also that the risk to the public may often outweigh the benefits to the prisoner of early release. Nonetheless, how the balance is to be struck remains a matter of judgement. The following case provides a classic example of this perennial tension between risk and trust:

Case 100: [SPO/HPO YES, RORS 14 per cent, RORA 25 per cent,[26] serving five years for causing grievous bodily harm with intent]

PBIM: *What impact has prison had on you?* Inmate: *This time it's hit me like a ton of bricks. I've missed the children, my family, friends. It's given me an insight into what problems I have caused. I know these circumstances won't arise again. I'm sure of myself. I know it won't happen again.*

The panel refused parole. Its **reasons** were: *His record reflects a serious pattern of offending over many years … Expressed remorse is welcome, but the panel considers that the risk of reoffending remains too high to grant an early release.*

Board members' satisfaction with the dossiers

Panel members were asked to rate their level of satisfaction with the most important reports in each dossier. Table 2.1 shows the proportion of reports which received at least one rating of dissatisfaction from a panel member and the proportion of prisoners who were paroled.[27]

Table 2.1: **Number and percentage of reports rated as satisfactory or unsatisfactory by at least one panel member and parole rate where reports were rated unsatisfactory**

Report	Number assessed	Percentage unsatisfactory	Unsatisfactory percentage paroled	Satisfactory percentage paroled
Psychiatric	45	38	18	29
Police	272	36	29	30
Prison parole assessment (PPA)	396	23	21	38
Course reports	186	22	27	45
HPO report (PAR)	391	22	23	37
SPO report	396	15	17	37

Table 2.1 reveals that – when provided – at least a third of police and psychiatric reports provoked dissatisfaction from at least one panel member. Most of those critical of police reports were concerned about the lack of detailed information on the circumstances of the offence. 'Superficiality' was the criticism most often aimed at unsatisfactory psychiatric reports.

---

26   The use that has been made in this research of Risk of Reconviction Scores (ROR) is discussed in Chapter 4 below. RORS refers to the risk of reconviction of a serious offence during the period available for parole licence. RORA refers to the risk of being convicted of any offence during the parole period. SPO/HPO YES (or NO) refers to the recommendations made by the seconded and home probation officers.

27   Views on the PBIM report are considered in Chapter 7.

There was much less dissatisfaction with probation officers' reports. The minority that were regarded as unsatisfactory were usually said to have provided an inadequate assessment of risk or, in the case of home probation officers, no proper release plan. Where a course report was criticised, it was usually because details of the nature of the course and the prisoner's response to it were lacking. Examples of such criticisms were:

Case 348: [SPO NO, HPO YES, RORS 6 per cent, RORA 14 per cent. The panel said NO]

The HPO wrote in his conclusions: *Mr X's friendly attitude and previous successful response to supervision augurs well for the future.*

Criminologist member: *The PAR glosses over or ignores risk factors identified and discussed by the SPO. The report writer was side-tracked by the friendly demeanour of the inmate.*

Case 352: [SPO/HPO YES, RORS 25 per cent, RORA 45 per cent. The panel said NO]

Independent member 1: *The HPO is very over-optimistic, poor risk assessment, written without seeing him, very poor practice.*

Independent member 2: *Mr X was not interviewed face-to-face for one-and-a- half years due to 'budget restrictions'. It's not fair to him or acceptable to the system.*

Case 60: [SPO/HPO YES, RORS 18 per cent, RORA 32 per cent. The panel said NO]

Probation member: *The course report says very little about the course and fails to give a clear picture of how he performed.*

As far as the dossiers as a whole were concerned, the majority of panel members had no complaint to make. But 20 per cent were described by at least one panel member as being poorly organised, 18 per cent were said to contain superfluous information, and a quarter were, at least in part, said to be illegible (mostly due to poor photocopying).

Table 2.1 also shows that (with the exception of police reports) where at least one panel member expressed dissatisfaction with a report, the parole rate was lower than when no member was dissatisfied. Thus, only 23 per cent of the prisoners with an 'unsatisfactory' home probation officer's report were paroled compared with 37 per cent of prisoners where the report was regarded as satisfactory. Similarly, the parole rate was considerably lower for those prisoners who had an unsatisfactory course report. This may have been as much a reflection on the quality of the course as on the reporting of the prisoner's response to it. Nevertheless, these data suggest that unsatisfactory reports may disadvantage parole applicants and provide another strong reason for trying to ensure that as few dossiers as possible fail to meet the expectations of those who have to rely on them when making decisions which affect the liberty of prisoners.

Delays

The majority of the 438 applicants for parole in this study (88%) were being considered for release for the first time. In a fifth of these cases (21%) the panel date was already later than the date at which the prisoner had been eligible for parole. Twenty-eight per cent of these prisoners were granted parole (they accounted for six per cent of all the first reviews). If these prisoners were released two days after the panel meeting (usually the minimum time) they would have spent, on average, 28 days longer in prison than was 'necessary'. Assuming that the sample was reasonably representative of delays occurring over the year as a whole, approximately 310 prisoners released at first review in 1998-99 would have had their parole applications delayed beyond their parole eligibility date (PED) for an average of 28 days. This is equivalent to 24 prisoner years, which would cost the prison service around £550,000. In addition, nearly 10 per cent of those released at a second or subsequent review had been considered after the anniversary date of their PED, the average delay being 82 days. On an annual basis such delays would add a further 16 prisoner years at a cost of around £370,000. The total cost would therefore be not far short of a million pounds a year.[28]

The reasons for delays in the parole process were analysed (as far as possible, given the information in the dossiers) in relation to cases where the delay beyond the prisoner's parole eligibility date was not obviously due to a decision made by the prisoner. Nearly all were delayed because the dossier arrived so late at the Parole Board Secretariat that it had not been possible to make up for the lost time.[29]

In just over a quarter of these 85 cases (28%), the delay occurred because the home probation officer's report had been very late arriving at the prison. The Sentence Enforcement Unit (formerly the Parole Unit) of the Prison Service is taking steps to deal with this. Chief Probation Officers have been made aware of the problems caused by the late receipt of home probation officers' reports and the new National Standards will include the target of sending such reports to the prison at least 13 weeks before the prisoner's parole eligibility date.[30]

Another quarter of delays appeared to have been due to failure to carry out the PBIM interview on time. In some cases this may have been because there was a shortage of interviewing members living in the region in which the prison was situated. New members have recently been recruited for such areas in order to try to combat delays in arranging interviews, and the Parole Board Secretariat has taken over, from parole clerks, responsibility for arranging PBIM interviews. Furthermore, from January 1999, parole clerks were given an extra week (and a further week from October 1999) to collate the dossier before having to send it to the Board's Secretariat.

---

28   According to a preliminary study carried out by the National Audit Office in 1999, serious delays in 1996-97 'resulted in more than 800 prisoners being kept in custody after their parole release date at an estimated cost of some £1.7m'. The figure was taken from a study conducted by Mike Shepherd (1998). Our figure may well be an underestimate because of the slightly lower parole rate for cases in our sample than for the year as a whole.

29   It has recently been proposed by the Parole Unit that a 'performance target' be set to ensure that 80 per cent of dossiers are received by the Parole Board Secretariat on time. Unforeseen or unavoidable delays are considered to make a higher percentage target unachievable.

30   H.M. Prison Service, *Parole Newsletter*, No. 4, Spring 1999, p. 2.

It was not easy in the remaining half of the cases to pinpoint, from the information in the dossier, the specific reasons for the delay.[31] It would be helpful if a full explanation of the reasons for delay were to be provided by the parole clerk in each case.

Delays have haunted the parole system. It will be important to see to what extent the new measures are successful in bringing about a permanent reduction in their incidence. Undue delays are, of course, an injustice to prisoners who suffer loss of liberty beyond the period at which the law allows them to be released when they have met the parole criteria.

---

31   For example, a prisoner may have been transferred between establishments during the parole process (a practice which the Parole Unit has tried to discourage), but it was not possible to know whether this in itself was the reason for the delay.

Chapter 3   At the Board

Who made the decisions?

When the Parole Board was established in 1967 it met in panels which reflected, as far as possible, the multi-disciplinary nature of the Board's statutory membership: judges, psychiatrists, probation officers, criminologists, and independent members drawn from different walks of life, many of whom had experience of working, in a professional or voluntary capacity, with the criminal justice system. Originally the Chairman and 16 members were appointed, including two or three from each of the statutory categories. They met in panels usually consisting of six members, with a representative from each constituency. Panels were later reduced to four members.[32] By 1971, the increasing number of cases under consideration had led to a doubling of the Board's size. Since then, the membership has continued to grow: to 85 in 1992 and by mid-1999 to 106.

The Carlisle Committee expected that once the new system had come fully into effect the number of Board members could 'be considerably reduced'.[33] But this has not been the case for a number of reasons:

- First, prisoners sentenced to four years' imprisonment were included in the DCR scheme, whereas Carlisle suggested that it should apply only to those sentenced to more than four years.

- Second, the long-term prison population has grown.

- Third, Parole Board members have had to be recruited to make it possible to interview prisoners in establishments around the country.

- Fourth, judicial and psychiatric members, plus a third member from another constituency, now deal with Discretionary Lifer Panels, so much so that judges (who chair the DLPs) no longer sit on determinate sentence panels.

- Fifth, psychiatrists now sit only on specially convened 'psychiatric panels' which deal with cases that have been identified by PBIMs as requiring a 'psychiatric input'. In an attempt to counterbalance these pressures, the quorum for a parole panel was reduced to three members in 1993, and in the same year six full-time salaried members were appointed (although by 1999 the number had been reduced to two).

---

32   See West (1972), at pp. 14-15
33   Carlisle (1998), para. 366.

Together, these changes have had a marked effect on the mix of qualifications of those who make up Parole Board panels. In the authors' study of Board decision-making in 1993-94, only three of the 24 panels observed (13%) consisted entirely of independent members. By 1999, 14 of the 36 panels (39%) at which tracked prisoners were considered were composed entirely of independents. 'Experts' (criminologists, probation officers and psychiatrists) outnumbered independents (two to one) on only three panels.[34] For the vast majority of prisoners, therefore, the decision was made by a panel where independent members – of varying backgrounds[35] – were in the majority.

No doubt the increase in the proportion of independent members on the Parole Board has been necessary in order to provide sufficient personnel to carry out the task of interviewing all candidates for parole. It is also worth noting that the Carlisle Committee was concerned to preserve the inter-disciplinary nature of panels and feared that this would be impaired if they were reduced to three members.[36]

How the panels went about their business

The three Board members who form a panel each receive 24 dossiers well in advance of the meeting. They are expected over a period of up to two days to read all 24 but, at the panel meeting, each is designated to 'lead' the discussion on eight cases and to prepare reasons in accordance with their initial decision, be it YES or NO. Sometimes (but in only five per cent of the observed cases in our sample) lead members took the precaution of drafting both YES and NO reasons. This was usually because it was recognised that the case for or against parole was not clear-cut and the lead member wanted to be prepared should the decision be contrary to the one he or she inclined towards.[37] One of the three panel members (who has been especially trained for the job) takes responsibility for chairing the panel and for recording the reasons and licence conditions which have been agreed. However, other than offering guidance on procedure and on how the discussion should be conducted, the Chair has no special role in the decision-making process.

At the majority of panels observed (11/20), the Chair indicated that he or she favoured what has become known as a 'bottom-line' approach. This involved going straight to the recommendation. Thus 'bottom-lining' usually took the form of an immediate: 'My bottom-line is NO [or YES]'. Sometimes there might be the briefest of introductions, such as: 'Mr A is aged 23, serving four years for burglary at Lindholme in category C, my bottom-line is NO [or YES]'. Typical comments by chairpersons were:

> The shorter the better. Bottom-line perhaps. If there is disagreement, there can be a full discussion of the case.

---

34   An independent member chaired 26 of the 36 panels. Furthermore, whereas in 1993-94 a full-time Parole Board member sat on 10 of the 24 panels, in 1999 full-time members sat on only four of the 36 panels.

35   Including, for example, teachers, voluntary workers, magistrates, prison visitors, former police officers, solicitors and local government employees. When independent members were recruited in 1999, they were specifically required to have 'a working knowledge' of the criminal justice system.

36   Carlisle (1988), para. 367.

37   Even so, in only four of these 20 cases were the lead member's preferences not followed.

Let's have a brief introduction and then go to the bottom-line and read out the reasons. Where we do have an iffy one we will go through the details.

Bottom-lining was relatively rare at seven of the 20 panels, where the lead member usually gave a much fuller introduction to the case under review.

The lead member took a 'bottom line' approach in 58 per cent of the observed cases. Thus a 'full introduction' was provided in just over four out of ten cases. Sometimes, lead members used introductions to remind themselves and other panel members of the basic facts in the dossier. On other occasions, lead members would concentrate on what they saw as the risk 'enhancers' and risk 'diminishers'. But there was no common approach. It was largely a matter of personal preference. Whichever approach was taken, lead members almost always made their preference clear (in 99% of cases), albeit occasionally using tentative words such as 'I'm an iffy YES' or 'I'm a NO but could be persuaded'.

The extent of agreement and dissent

Now that panels have just three members there is no possibility of a panel failing to reach a decision, even if that decision is to defer the case to obtain more information. Nor is there a formal way of registering dissent: the minority member has to accept the 'cabinet' decision. A member with a minority view can only get it accepted if one of the others is willing to change his or her mind. Where the other two firmly state their position, it is rarely worth a third member arguing for long. Table 3.1 shows the number of observed cases in which disagreement resulted in a different final decision from that expressed initially by the lead member; and the number in which panel members ultimately confirmed the decision that the lead member had initially suggested. It can be seen that:

- In eight out of every ten cases the lead member's initial preference was followed by the other two members, with neither of them voicing dissent.

- In a further 10 per cent of cases it was confirmed after some dissent and discussion.

Furthermore:

- In the minority of cases where the lead member's initial preference was changed or overruled, it was usually the result of the combined influence of the other two members of the panel.

- In only five instances did one dissenting panel member persuade at least one of the other members to change their mind, and always from a YES to a NO; never from NO to YES.

Table 3.1:   Final decision related to lead member's initial preference

Lead member's preference	Number	Percentage
YES confirmed with no dissent	115	27.6
NO confirmed with no dissent	225	53.9
Total: Lead YES or NO confirmed without dissent	340	81.5
YES confirmed after dissent and discussion	19	4.6
NO confirmed after dissent and discussion	23	5.5
Total YES or NO preferences confirmed	382	91.6
YES or DEFER changed to NO	22	5.3
NO changed to YES	9	2.1
Total lead preferences changed or overruled	31	7.4
Lead member uncertain (Final decision YES 1, NO 3)	4	1.0
TOTAL	417	100

Thus, the cases considered by the panels observed generated some discussion arising from a disagreement by one or more members in relation to only 73 prisoners (18%). For 42 of these prisoners (58%), discussion did not change the initial recommendation, while for 31 prisoners (42%) it did. These changed decisions, which accounted for just over seven per cent of all the decisions taken, were not evenly distributed between the panels: for example, a third of the changes (11) occurred at two of the 20 panels, whereas at eight panels no changes occurred.

A rare example where a lead member's NO preference was overruled was:

Case 209: [SPO/HPO YES, RORS 5%, RORA 12%, serving five years for robbery]

Independent member (lead): *He's aged 24, at X Prison. This is a drugs and alcohol related offence. A robbery when he was on bail. It was a series of robberies, carried out at knifepoint at cash dispensers. My bottom-line is NO. He's not ready to go yet.* The two other members (a criminologist and an independent) both said YES. The lead replied: *He's got 48 [extra] days inside. The offences arose from severe bouts of drinking, using cannabis, speed and heroin. He's not a habitual, serious offender, but he did use a knife.* Independent: *I will discount early possession offences.* Criminologist: *I felt continuing supervision was more criminogenic. He's not, by any means, a calculating, determined offender. When challenged immediately by victims, he didn't raise the ante. He's one who's had a previous unblemished character. He was caught for common assault and criminal damage. He's done the course work. He hasn't got an anti-social profile. He's vulnerable but not a criminal young man.* Lead: *There have been problems inside involving cannabis brought in by a visitor.* Criminologist: *If anything emerges, a further charge, that will put a different complexion on it. He's going to a new area and I felt that if he stays in his old area, he's in danger from one of the victims.*

Independent: *I had that he had no criminal record. He handed himself in to the police.* Lead: *The reasons underlying his offending worry me. They haven't been explored.* Criminologist: *He got into heavy drinking and wanted to fund it.* Lead: *So you think going to his father – or is it his uncle – without employment will be alright?* Independent: *If he does it again, he'll get life.*

Reasons: The final sentence in the lead member's original draft of the Reasons **had** read: *The Panel, however, consider that further work needs to be done on the causes and consequences of offending, in particular on anger and drugs in order to reduce the risk he presents to an acceptable level. Parole is refused.* This was **changed** to: *The Panel consider that the risk of offending has been reduced to an acceptable level and that further offence–related work can be better carried out during a longer period of supervision.*

Time taken

As mentioned above, panel members spend up to two days prior to the meeting reading the 24 dossiers that will be discussed, making notes, and drafting reasons for the eight cases on which they will lead the discussion. This must be borne in mind when considering the time taken to decide cases at the panel meetings. Of the decisions observed, 57 per cent were reached in four minutes or less (including reading of the reasons and discussion of licence conditions). There was little difference in this regard whether the Board reached a YES or a NO decision. The time taken to deal with each case largely depended on the approach taken by the lead member and on whether disagreement arose. Indeed, where all members agreed and where the lead went to the 'bottom-line', either straight away or after a brief introduction, nearly 90 per cent of cases were dealt with within four minutes. On the other hand, where the lead member gave a lengthy introduction, only four out of ten were completed in four minutes or less, and nearly a quarter (24%) took eight minutes or more. Where there was disagreement, six out of ten discussions took eight minutes or longer. It is interesting to note that the lead member's approach, to use either a bottom-line or a full introduction, made no difference to the proportion granted parole.[38]

How often was parole granted?

The proportion of prisoners released on parole in our sample of 438 cases was 33.6 per cent, rather lower than the 39.6 per cent for all DCR cases dealt with by the Board in 1998-99. To some extent this is accounted for by the higher proportion of sex offenders in our sample (21%) compared with the proportion dealt with over the year as a whole, which was 15 per cent. On the other hand, the release rate for sex offenders was higher in our sample (20%) compared with 12 per cent over the whole year. The researchers also observed a slightly higher proportion of 'psychiatric panels' than would be expected and this had some effect because psychiatric panels paroled only 26 per cent of prisoners

---

38   Percentage paroled: 'bottom-line' 33 per cent; full introduction 36.5 per cent (this was not statistically significant).

compared with 37 per cent paroled by non-psychiatric panels.[39] Nevertheless, when the proportion of cases in our sample was 'weighted', so as to reflect the proportion in each offence group in the national annual statistics, the release rate was equivalent to 38.4 per cent, virtually the same as the national figure.

As pointed out above (page 4), the Carlisle Committee intended that the new scheme would raise the rate at which parole was granted rather than lower it. What has happened? There are four reasons why it is difficult to compare the Board's paroling rate in the current DCR sample, with the rate at which the Board was granting parole to a sample gathered under the 'old parole system'. First, under the old system prisoners were eligible after serving a third of their sentence. Now, all prisoners have to serve half their sentence before being considered for parole. Second, all prisoners serving a sentence of four years or more used to receive at least two parole reviews, whereas now two-thirds of prisoners (those serving less than six-and-a-half years) receive only one review. Third, formerly the only way by which prisoners could be released under statutory supervision was to grant them parole, whereas under the DCR system all prisoners are subject to supervision even if not released on parole. Fourth, under the old system, prisoners who were not recommended for parole by the Local Review Committee (LRC) and who had a Reconviction Prediction Score of more than 45 per cent were not referred to the Board for consideration unless it was their last review.[40] In contrast, under the DCR system, the Board now deals with all prisoners, irrespective of their risk.

For these reasons, the proportion of prisoners who received parole at some time prior to having served two-thirds of their sentence is the only meaningful comparison that can be made between the 'old system' and DCR. The *Report of the Parole Board for 1994* shows that, at some point in their sentence, 69.7 per cent of prisoners, serving four years or more under the old system, who were reviewed between June 1992 and May 1995, were released on parole before serving two-thirds of their sentence.[41] The latest *Report of the Parole Board for 1998/99* reveals that 47.7 per cent of all prisoners dealt with under the DCR system from its inception until March 1999 have been granted parole.[42] Thus:

- The percentage paroled at some time has fallen by 22 percentage points.

- This is equivalent to a 32 per cent lower paroling rate.

There are three factors that might explain the decline in the parole rate. One, of course, is the tightening of the risk criteria set out in the Secretary of State's directions and the way in

39   Although the proportion of sex offenders released by psychiatric and non-psychiatric panels was virtually the same: 19.1 per cent compared with 20.8 per cent.

40   A few other high-risk prisoners were referred to the Board: all women, a prisoner whose co-defendant had been referred, and a prisoner deemed unsuitable by a LRC by only a three to two majority. This filter mechanism ceased to be applied to old system cases whose PED (or its anniversary) was after 1 October 1994.

41   Parole Board (1995), Table 12, p. 33. It was in this year that a calculation was first made of the proportion of prisoners who had been paroled at any time during their sentence. It was the nearest we could get to the rate under the 'old system'. These cases were reviewed after the 'restricted policy' had been rescinded in June 1992. It had restricted the granting of parole to prisoners serving more than five years for an offence of sex, violence or drugs to, at most, the last few months available.

42   Parole Board (1999). The relevant table is to be found on p. 49.

which panel members have interpreted these directions. Another is the fact that the Parole Board no longer has to grant parole if it wishes to ensure that the prisoner will be supervised on release from prison. A third arises from the fact that most prisoners under the DCR scheme only get one review and therefore, if granted parole, have to be given a relatively long period on parole licence (at least eight months for a person sentenced to four years). For those who are perceived to be higher risks, this may be regarded as too long. In contrast, under the old system, where all long-term prisoners received at least two reviews, the Board could, and often did, control risk by releasing higher risk prisoners at their last review for relatively short periods of parole. These factors must be borne in mind when interpreting the findings of this research.

Reasons for refusing parole

Risk, of course, is now the Board's overriding consideration. Indeed, 97 per cent of reasons given for refusal in the sample of cases in this study included a sentence to the effect that 'the risk of reoffending is too high for release on licence'. However:

- In 84 per cent of cases the reasons mentioned specific indicators of risk, such as the seriousness of the offence, a previous history of sexual or violent offending, previous failure to respond to supervision and breaches of bail or 'breaches of trust' while on temporary licence from prison.

- In 96 per cent mention was made of failure to address, or make sufficient progress in addressing, offending behaviour, either generally or in relation to specific areas of concern, such as drugs, anger, alcohol or sex offending. This included 37 per cent in which mention was made of poor prison behaviour.

- In only 29 per cent was an inadequate release plan mentioned and in only a handful of cases poor employment prospects or unfavourable domestic circumstances.

Failure in relation to all three of the above factors was mentioned in 23 per cent of cases, failure on two grounds in 63 per cent, and on one ground only in 14 per cent.

Addressing offending behaviour

Of particular interest is the Board's response in cases where members identified 'failure to address, or make sufficient progress in addressing, offending behaviour' as a reason for refusal. There is obviously a danger that prisoners who, through no fault of their own, are unable to obtain a place on a course or complete it in time for their parole review, will be disadvantaged. If such weight is to be given to offending-behaviour courses, it is vital that they should be available to all prisoners who seek them and that prisoners should be in a position to complete them in good time before a parole reviews begins. In addition, there should be intelligible rating scales so that a prisoner's performance can be objectively judged, and there should be an explanation when courses regarded as essential have not been undertaken or completed. Above all, the effectiveness of behavioural-change programmes in prison needs to be regularly evaluated in comparison with their effectiveness when provided as part of parole supervision in the community.[43]

There is evidence to suggest that panel members believed that courses carried out in prison were likely to be efficacious. In almost a third of the cases refused parole the panel stressed that 'more work' should be done in prison before the prisoner was released – or sometimes that the work done should be 'consolidated' during a further period of custody.[44]

Case 58: [SPO/HPO YES, RORS 9%, RORA 22%, serving four years for possession of cocaine]

Independent member (lead): *He's on a drug-free spur in prison. His last prison offence was [seven months prior to the panel] and he's been drug-free since then.* Probation member: *A three-day drug course for a raving drug user is not going to change him.* The lead member changed her mind and the panel refused parole.

Reasons: … *Whilst changes are noted, he has a poor history of recidivism and breaches of trust. The panel considers that he remains too high a risk for release until further work is completed.*

Case 406: [SPO/HPO YES, RORS 7%, RORA 10%, serving eight years for indecent assault and at his second review]

Psychiatrist member: *There's been a very long period of abuse. He suddenly does the Sex Offender Treatment Programme (SOTP) and then he does wonderfully well. These things don't tally. There's little victim empathy. Then comes the SOTP with good victim empathy. He needs to continue to work on the SOTP and then after that.*

In two-thirds of the cases where panel members thought that 'more work' should be done in prison, one of the probation officers (and usually both of them) had recommended release on parole. This was probably because they considered that the longer period of supervision on parole licence would be more likely to reduce the risk than if the prisoner were to remain in custody. Any resolution of this difference of opinion needs to take into account the findings of research. The evidence available so far suggests that, in general (there will always be exceptions), the effectiveness of offending behaviour programmes is enhanced when they are undertaken in the community rather than in custody and that 'having adjusted for risk factors, those released on parole still have lower rates of reconviction than those not

---

43   On the influence of completion of offending-behaviour courses on the parole decision see Table 4.4, page 42 below.
44   Ninety one of the 280 cases (32.5%) where 'failure to address offending behaviour etc' was mentioned in the reasons for refusal, and 91 of all 291 refusals (31.3%).

paroled'.[45] In deciding what risks to take, members of the Board will be assisted if they are kept up-to-date with the evidence on the comparative effectiveness of prison and community based programmes as they emerge from the government's crime reduction programme.

Denial

A longstanding and difficult issue for the Parole Board is how to respond to those who deny that they were guilty of the offence. There were 54 'deniers' in our sample. Thirty-seven of them were sex offenders, of whom only two were granted parole.

In a landmark case in 1995, arising from judicial review of a decision by the Board, it was held that a prisoner's application for parole should not be refused on the sole ground that he denied the offence.[46] Panel members are therefore warned to be circumspect in the way they express their reasons when denial is obviously a factor affecting their view that the prisoner has not satisfactorily 'addressed his or her offending behaviour'.

Case 28: [HPO/SPO NO, RORS 2%, RORA 2%, serving four years for rape of a former employee]

The lead member (new Independent) read her **Reasons** for refusal: ... *He has steadfastly laid blame on the victim, denied his offence, and refused to undertake any SOTP. As a result of his attitude and lack of attendance at relevant offence-related courses, the Board feel that his risk of reoffending is still too high to warrant early release.* Chair (Probation member): *They don't like us saying denying the offence. They like not addressing offending behaviour.* Lead: *Why? What's the difference?* Chair: *You had better ask the judges. In relation to judicial reviews the reasons have to be properly framed.*[47]

The revised **Reasons** substituted: ... *He has failed to adequately address the causes and consequences of such offending. Further, there is little to suggest that he has made use of his time in custody to pursue educational and skills courses to prepare himself for release.*

Case 226: [HPO/SPO YES, RORS 14%, RORA 17%, serving ten years for incest, indecent assault and buggery, third review]

Psychiatrist: ... *He pleaded not guilty to all these [sexual] offences and continues to maintain his innocence ... I have to be careful about my reasons, because of the*

---

45   Vennard and Hedderman (1998), at p. 104 and pp. 109-110. See also Ellis and Marshall (1998), pp. 43-50, who found a statistically significant difference between the actual proportion of paroled prisoners reconvicted (26%) over a follow-up period of two years, and the proportion predicted to be reconvicted (28%) on the basis of their characteristics. This difference of two percentage points is equivalent to a seven per cent lower rate of reconviction for paroled prisoners.

46   *R v The Secretary of State for the Home Department, ex parte Mohammed Zulfikar* [1996] C.O.D. 256, also *The Times* 26 July 1995. This was recently confirmed by the High Court in the review of the Board's refusal to grant parole to Owen Oyston on the grounds of his persistent denial of the sex offences of which he was convicted. See *R v The Secretary of State for the Home Department, ex parte Owen Oyston* (unreported, but see *The Independent*, 15 October 1999).

47   It should be noted that in *Zulfikar*, the Divisional Court criticised the use of the expression 'addressing his offending behaviour' when the prisoner denied the offence, as a 'piece of jargon'. See Parole Board (1996), para. 17.

warning we have had that not addressing one's offending behaviour and protesting one's innocence as a reason is appealable.

Reasons *... Mr X has consistently denied his part in the index offences and has declined to participate in sex offender treatment programmes or on work exploring violent offending. In the absence of such work the panel looked for other indications of progress. There was, however, no evidence that he had gained insight into his offending or into the trauma he inflicted on his victim ...*

However, denial was not a virtual bar to parole for the 16 non-sex offenders, seven (44%) of whom were released, three of them having denied importing illegal drugs.

Case 356: *[SPO/HPO YES, RORS 0%, RORA 1%, serving four years six months for importing cannabis]*

Independent member (lead): I said yes ... He was adamant that he didn't know it was cannabis ... He has no previous convictions ... He has no adjudications. He was assessed not to be in need of thinking skills courses. He's been working outside. He is recommended by both the probation officers. There's not much else we could ask him to do. Second Independent: Well he's done no offence work. Lead: But he's not an addict or supplier in the true sense ... Second Independent: We ought to be consistent if they don't do the courses. Third Independent (Chair): But he's in category D. Lead: I couldn't think of any conditions that were necessary. This sentence will be the deterrent. The prison probation officer says he will not reoffend ... I'm quite happy with this, particularly looking at nine months on parole.

The link between denial and risk of reconviction, both for sex and non-sex offenders, is analysed in Chapter 4.

Receiving reasons for refusal

More than eight out of ten of the refused prisoners who were interviewed thought the reasons they had been given were unfair. Half said they had found them 'hard to take'. Three-quarters said that they had not changed their behaviour in response to the reasons given and, of the quarter who said they had changed, most (at least three-quarters) claimed to have reacted negatively. The following comments were typical:

I was off drugs for 12 months. As soon as I got my knock back I went back on them [cannabis and tablets]. Nowt to lose now.

I started skinning up. You don't give a fuck after a knock back. They can't give you no more bird.

These responses can, of course, be interpreted in a variety of ways. One is that the prospect of parole encourages good behaviour and refusal encourages bad behaviour. Another is that these men had never been genuine in their desire to address their offending behaviour. Whichever is the case, it seems clear that the Board's attempt to communicate to prisoners, through reasons for refusal, what changes they needed to make to their behaviour prior to their release, did not meet with a positive response.

Reasons for granting parole

It was not surprising to find that reasons for granting parole almost always reflected a judgement that risk was sufficiently low to warrant early release. Board members also mentioned in almost all their reasons (98%) that the prisoner had made an effort to 'address his offending behaviour'. In a third of YES reasons the panel drew attention to prisoners' expressions of remorse or regret for their offending behaviour.

There appears to have been a change since panels were observed by the authors in 1993-94. Then, 'progress in addressing offending behaviour' was mentioned in only two-thirds of the reasons for granting parole, even though the 1992 directions required the Board to be satisfied that such progress had been made. There are two possible explanations of why the Board now mentions this factor more often than it did in the past. First, it may be more conscious of the need to ensure that its reasons match the Secretary of State's directions: new members are told that to make sure that this is done is 'perhaps the single most important factor' when drafting reasons.[48] A second possibility is that the change reflects the revival of a belief in the rehabilitative possibilities of imprisonment, but now linked to a risk-assessment agenda. Perhaps both are at work.

Tracked prisoners who were coming up to their parole review, as well as refused prisoners (who had of course already been given reasons), were asked what the Parole Board took into account when deciding whether or not to grant parole. It is interesting to note that nearly six out of ten of both groups failed to mention that they needed 'to address their offending behaviour', for example by taking and doing well on offending behaviour courses. Thus, in this regard, there seems to be a serious gap in communication between the Board, the Prison Service and prisoners.

Panels mentioned that the prisoner had a 'satisfactory release plan' in 73 per cent of the instances where they granted parole. On the other hand, in only 30 per cent of cases paroled was it said that the risk would be 'further reduced by a period of supervision under parole licence', or words to that effect. This reinforces the impression that members of the Board do not have a great deal of confidence in the effectiveness of parole supervision as such.

---

48 Terry McCarthy, 'Reasons to be Cheerful' (an abridged version of a session given during new member training), *Parole Board News* (the Board's Newsletter), No. 7, September 1999.

Licence conditions

The average period of parole licence granted to the 147 paroled prisoners was 330 days.[49] The shortest period anyone gained was 50 days and the longest 775 days. The Annual Reports of the Parole Board show that the average licence period is rather longer for DCR cases granted parole than it was for long-term prisoners under the old system: around 13 months compared with about 11 months.[50]

Eighty-seven per cent of those paroled had a condition attached to their licence, whereas, before the introduction of the DCR scheme, it was found that conditions were attached in half as many cases (44%).[51] Of those prisoners in the present study who were paroled:

- Fifty-two per cent had a residence condition attached to their licence compared with 15 per cent under the old system.

- The proportion released on condition that they continue to address their offending behaviour (including drugs, alcohol, anger and sex) was 82 per cent compared with 32 per cent under the old system.

Since most of those paroled had already satisfactorily completed offending behaviour courses while in custody, adding more 'treatment conditions' during supervision probably reflected a belief that the parole licence period should be made more stringent. Indeed, 44 per cent of those paroled had three or more conditions attached to their licence. Whether or not it is realistic to expect so many conditions to be fulfilled by the prisoner and provided and enforced by the probation service are issues worthy of research.

The DCR scheme ensures that a prisoner who is not paroled but released at the two-thirds point of the sentence (NPD) is also subject to supervision. The Carlisle Committee, which recommended that it should be possible to attach conditions to those released at their NPD, thought that:

> In practice the scope for the Parole Board to set individualised conditions for those denied release until the two-thirds point is bound to be more limited than for those released earlier who will have much more of an incentive to comply with the requirements tailored for them.[52]

---

49 The median period of parole licence was 316 days. The figures refer to the parole licence: i.e. from release on parole to the two-thirds point (NPD) of the sentence. The Report of the Parole Board for 1998-99 reveals that the total average length of licence for all DCR prisoners released on parole in 1998/99 – i.e. from date of release to the three-quarters point of the sentence – was 15.4 months (approximately 462 days), see Parole Board (1999), p. 45.

50 Old system prisoners were paroled both earlier and later in their sentence than are DCR cases. Among the cases observed in 1993-94, 38 per cent were being considered by the Board at their first review, after serving one-third of the sentence: 32 per cent of them were paroled. On the other hand, 62 per cent were at their last review, which in nearly all cases would have been beyond the half-way point of their sentence. Of the 70 per cent of them paroled, many had a relatively short period of licence. In comparison, most prisoners reviewed under the DCR system have only 'one shot' at parole after serving a half of their sentence: they either get the full period on licence available between that time and two-thirds of their sentence, or nothing.

51 Hood and Shute (1994), p.58. It was still 43 per cent in 1993-94, see Hood and Shute (1995), p. 35.

52 Carlisle (1998), para. 383.

However, the Board has proved to be much more vigorous in its use of licence conditions than Carlisle anticipated. In 97 per cent of the cases in this study where panels denied parole to a prisoner at last review, an offending behaviour condition (and in 62% a residence condition) was attached to the NPD licence. Six out of ten had three or more conditions.

Sixty-six of the interviewed prisoners who had recently been refused parole voiced an opinion about their NPD licence. Only ten of them were favourably disposed and 38 (58%) were very negative. Indeed, 28 (42%) considered it unreasonable to place such conditions on a person who had been refused parole and were adamant that they would not comply:

Silly and spurious. They can shove them up their arse. They can't force me to do it. It's just nonsense.

When I go the Parole Board hasn't got a hope in hell of getting me to do anything. I'd rather do the full six years than let them tell me what I have to do. If they'd given me parole they could've set conditions. They haven't given me anything. They had the chance to lay down conditions and they fluffed it.

I'll ignore them. They're bollocks. It's damn cheeky of them. If they want to keep me in for four months fine … They're trying to extend their powers. Who are they to tell me where to live?

It may be that these responses show that such prisoners were indeed too great a risk to trust on a parole licence. But they may also underline a more serious problem of trying to enforce licence conditions on ex-prisoners who believe that if they have to be on licence they should have been trusted on parole. Indeed, their sense of frustration may be better understood when it is realised that, as will be shown later (page 51 below), a sizeable minority of those refused parole had their hopes dashed after being recommended for it by both the seconded and home probation officers.

It would be a useful project to investigate whether such widespread hostility to NPD licence conditions from those who fail to benefit from the parole system is translated in reality into enforcement difficulties for the probation service.[53]

---

53   It is interesting to note that 71 per cent of 42 ex-prisoners interviewed for a study of Automatic Conditional Release said that the licence conditions had placed no significant restrictions on them and 64 per cent said that it had had no effect at all on their behaviour. On the other hand, the majority had been favourably disposed to their supervising officer. See Maguire, Peroud and Raynor (1996), pp. 68-71. Since this report was published attempts have been made to ensure that ACR licences are more stringently enforced. From 1 January 1999 responsibility for the recall of offenders on ACR licences was passed to the Secretary of State on the recommendation of the Parole Board under section 103 of the Crime and Disorder Act 1991.

Chapter 4   Risk and the decision to grant or deny parole

As risk of committing further offences if released on parole licence is the primary consideration that the Board is directed to take into account, this chapter raises two questions. First, to what extent do release decisions reflect risk? Second, what degree of risk does the Board take when deciding to grant parole? The only means available at present of answering these questions is to gauge decision-making in relation to actuarial, objectively-determined, risk of reconviction data.

Predicting the risk of reconviction

Since the 1920s efforts have been made, beginning in the United States, to predict the probability of an inmate being reconvicted after release from prison. The purpose was to provide a 'base expectancy' probability of reconviction which could serve both as a guide when deciding who should be released on parole and as a standard against which the successful outcome of parole could be assessed. The first statistically sophisticated study in the UK was *Prediction Methods in Relation to Borstal Training*, published in 1955. In the 1970s the method was applied to the parole system by Christopher Nuttall and colleagues in the Home Office Research Unit. Their study showed that it was possible to produce a valid and reliable prediction score based on 16 variables relating to various offence-related, criminal history and social characteristics of the offender, which produced, for each prisoner, a percentage probability of being reconvicted within a two-year period of release from prison.[54] This prediction score was used by the Parole Board as a 'parity mechanism' to ensure that all prisoners with a probability of reconviction of 45 per cent or less were referred to the Board, whether they had been recommended for parole by the Local Review Committee or not. The reconviction prediction score (RPS)[55] was made available to Board members on the front of each prisoner's dossier but by the early 1990s was only available for those cases referred to the Board which the LRC had regarded as 'unsuitable'.[56]

With the advent of Discretionary Conditional Release for prisoners serving four years or more, it became necessary to calculate a new risk of reconviction score. This task was carried out by the distinguished statisticians John Copas, of the University of Warwick, and Peter Marshall and Roger Tarling of the Home Office Research, Development and Statistics Directorate. They calculated, on the basis of a sample of more than 1,200 long-term prisoners released from prison in 1987, both the probability of reconviction *during the parole period* ('when he or she would otherwise have been in custody') and over *a period of two years from release*. They also included, for each of these periods, a separate estimate of the likelihood of committing a serious offence – defined as 'one which resulted

---

54   Nuttall *et al.* (1977).
55   The RPS was kept under review and tested for its validity. See, Ward (1987).
56   For example, in a sample of cases observed at the Board in 1992, it was available on one-third of the dossiers, and in 1993-94 on 45 per cent. See Hood and Shute (1994), para. 175, and Hood and Shute (1995), paras 52-56.

in the imposition of a new custodial sentence'.[57] These distinctions were a response to the recommendations of the Carlisle Committee, which, it will be recalled, stated:

> The parole decision will … be based upon an evaluation of the risk to the public of the person committing a further serious offence at a time when he would otherwise be in prison …The risk to be assessed is whether a further serious offence might be committed. It would clearly not be right to prolong a person's detention for several months or even years simply on the strength of a fear that he could commit the sort of offence which would merit a non-custodial sentence or at most a short prison sentence.[58]

The directions under which Parole Board members made decisions at the time this study was undertaken similarly emphasised that the risk to be guarded against is 'at a time when the prisoner would otherwise be in prison'. However, they also stated that 'a risk of violent or sexual offending is more serious than the risk of other types of offending'. Thus, the prediction instrument developed by Copas, Marshall and Tarling estimates the risk of being reconvicted of a wider range of serious offences – any that would be expected to lead to imprisonment – than the narrower categories of offence to which the Board is directed to pay particular attention.

The Carlisle Committee stated emphatically that 'the Board should be under a duty to take into account statistical prediction techniques and, where appropriate, 'clinical' assessments, which will assist it in its work'.[59] Accordingly, the directions given to the Board in 1992 instructed members to take into account 'any available statistical indicators as to the likelihood of reoffending'. It became the policy of the Board to include a page in the dossier setting out the calculated ROR, which was disclosed to the prisoner. However, by the time the current study was undertaken, it had been decided to discontinue calculating prediction scores. It was felt that the resources required could not be justified, probably because the scores were rarely given a lot of weight in decision-making.[60] Indeed, the Board's *Policy and Procedures Manual* (dated September 1997), which included useful information for members about the ROR, warned them that it 'provides no more than a starting point for the consideration of risk in releasing an individual prisoner'. It also rightly points out that the ROR score is 'an average or expected outcome for all cases of that type'; it must 'be regarded as approximate … hence fine distinctions should not be drawn between one ROR and another'; it 'takes no account of offending which has gone undiscovered or may not have led to a conviction'; and 'it takes no account of factors *after* sentence which are important to the parole decision'. But this does not mean that prisoners with a low average risk of reconviction should not be considered as *prima facie* better prospects for parole than those with high average risks of reconviction.

For the purposes of this research the ROR was the only valid means available for studying to what extent the Board's decisions reflected risk of reconviction. The score made it possible to compare the parole rate of prisoners who, in aggregate, posed different average

---

57   Copas, Marshall and Tarling (1996).
58   Carlisle (1998), paras 321-322.
59   *Ibid.* para. 330.
60   In the authors' observations of panels in 1993-94, they found that, even when the prediction score was available on the dossier, it was not referred to in the discussion in nearly 60 per cent of cases. See Hood and Shute (1995), para. 53.

degrees of risk. The researchers therefore calculated, using the Copas programme, the ROR for each parole applicant in the sample of 438 cases,[61] distinguishing between the probability of reconviction of a serious offence during the available parole period (RORS) and reconviction of any offence over the same period (RORA). Calculations were also made of the risk of reconviction of a serious and of any offence over a two-year period.

Because of the importance in the directions attached to reoffending during the parole period, and the greater weight to be given to violent and sexual offending, the analysis that follows mainly uses the RORS score. As explained above, violent or sexual offending is a narrower criterion than the criterion of serious offending. This means that the RORS score will be higher – and the risk will look greater – than if the score were only estimating the risk of a reconviction for a violent or sexual offence.

Three points need to be emphasised. First, the ROR score refers only to *the risk of reconviction* not to the obviously greater risk of *reoffending*. It is, of course, impossible to make statistically reliable estimates of risk on the basis of unknown rates of reoffending, and most people would regard it as unjust to do so. However, it is known that there is a correlation between the rate of reoffending and the probability of reconviction. A reconviction prediction score is therefore likely also to discriminate between low and high risks of reoffending. Secondly, every study of the subject has shown that statistically-based *actuarial predictions* of reconviction are far more accurate in aggregate than *'clinical' predictions*, whoever they are made by.[62] Lastly, there is no reason to believe that the associations between factors and reconviction that Copas, Marshall and Tarling found in the large sample of prisoners they followed-up are no longer valid.[63] However, it might be possible to devise more accurate and discriminating prediction instruments, perhaps by the inclusion of 'dynamic factors' which measure the relationship between offenders' responses to treatment programmes and reconviction.[64]

The analyses which follow make use of the ROR score to show the correlation between actuarial risk of reconviction and parole outcomes (for a detailed analysis see Appendix 3). The cut-off point between low and high risk of reconviction for a serious offence on parole (RORS) reflects the level at which the parole rate changed markedly:

- Half the sample had a RORS of 7 per cent or below and half of them were paroled.

- In comparison, only 16 per cent of the half with a RORS of 8 per cent or above were paroled.

61   The authors are grateful to John Ditchfield for making the programme for calculating these scores available to us.
62   See Monahan and Steadman (1994), pp. 1-17.
63   The factors were: age at conviction, male or female, number of youth custody sentences, number of adult custodial sentences, number of previous convictions, and type of offence. A Home Office analysis of reconviction rates of males released from prison in 1987 and 1995 and sentenced to over four years has shown that the reconviction rate for any offence over a period of two years was the same (31%), as was the proportion sentenced to imprisonment during the same follow-up period (15%). This suggests that the ROR calculated from a sample of prisoners released in 1987 remains a valid indicator of the overall risk of reconviction. See Kershaw, Goodman and White (1999).
64   Such as the instrument called OASys, which the Home Office is developing.

Type of offence, ROR, and the parole rate

It is well known that the parole rate varies a good deal according to the type of offence for which a prisoner is convicted. As Table 4.1 shows, 77 per cent of prisoners in the sample of observed cases who had been convicted of importing drugs were paroled, as were 50 per cent of those convicted of other drug offences. On the other hand, only a fifth of those imprisoned for burglary or for a sex offence were paroled.

Table 4.1: Parole rates by main offence type and RORS score

Offence type	RORS	Average RORS	Number of cases	Percentage in risk band	Percentage paroled
Import drugs	0%–7%	1.7%	21	95.5	81.0
	8%+	11.0%	1	4.5	-
Total			22		77.3
Arson	0%–7%	2.5%	6	100	66.7
	8%+	-	-	-	-
Total			6		66.7
Other drug offences	0%–7%	2.9%	43	79.6	60.5
	8%+	13.9%	11	20.4	9.1
Total			54		50.0
Theft/handling/ fraud/deception	0%–7%	3.4%	9	47.4	66.6
	8%+	21.9%	10	52.6	10.0
Total			19		36.8
Personal violence	0%–7%	4.5%	40	43.5	52.5
	8%+	17.2%	52	56.5	19.2
Total			92		33.7
Robbery	0%–7%	5.0%	34	35.8	55.9
	8%+	17.6%	61	64.2	16.4
Total			95		30.5
Burglary	0%–7%	4.8%	10	18.9	50.0
	8%+	23.6%	43	81.1	14.0
Total			53		20.8
Sex offences	0%–7%	3.2%	59	64.1	22.0
	8%+	15.3%	33	35.9	15.2
Total			92		19.5
Other	0%–7%	1.7%	4	100	75.0
	8%+	-	-	-	-
			437*		33.6

* One case – a foreign national for whom a ROR could not be calculated – was excluded.

Table 4.1 also shows that much of the difference in parole rates of prisoners convicted of different types of offence can be explained by the proportion of them with a relatively low probability of being reconvicted for a serious offence while on parole (RORS). Thus, nearly all importers of drugs, compared with less than one in five of the burglars, were in the lowest RORS risk band. And the lower parole rate for the burglars in that risk band (50% compared with 81% of drug importers) can be partly explained by the fact that their average RORS score was 4.8 per cent compared with 1.7 per cent for drug importers.

However, the low parole rate for sex offenders cannot be explained in this way. Nearly two-thirds of sex offenders had a RORS of 7 per cent or less (average 3.2%), yet only 22 per cent of them were paroled. It is thus apparent that the relationship between RORS and the Board's decisions was different for sex offenders than for non-sex offenders. Parole decisions for sex offenders have therefore been analysed separately.

ROR and parole decisions

Tables 4.2 and 4.3 show (for non-sex offenders and sex offenders respectively) the relationship between the actuarial risk of reconviction for a serious offence during the time when the prisoner would otherwise have been in prison and the parole decision.

Table 4.2:   Relationship between ROR for a serious offence on parole licence and parole decision (non-sex offenders)

Actuarial RORS	Number of cases	Number and percentage paroled		Percentage of cases in each risk group
		Number	Percentage	
0%–2%	52	43	82.7	15.1
3%–7%	115	58	50.4	33.3
Total 0%–7%	167	101	60.5	48.4
8%–16%	100	22	22.0	29.0
17% and higher	78	6	7.7	22.6
Total 8% and higher	178	28	15.7	51.6
Total	345	129	37.4	100

Comparing percentage paroled for Total 0%–7% and Total 8% plus: $\chi^2 = 73.7$, 1df, p < 0.0001

Table 4.3: Relationship between ROR for a serious offence on parole licence and parole decision (sex offenders)

Actuarial RORS	Number of cases	Number and percentage paroled		Percentage of cases in each risk group
		Number	Percentage	
0%–2%	31	5	16.1	33.7
3%–7%	28	8	28.6	30.5
Total 0%–7%	59	13	22.0	64.2
8%–16%	24	4	16.7	26.1
17% and higher	9	1	11.1	9.8
Total 8% and higher	33	5	15.2	35.9
Total	92	18	19.6	100

Comparing percentage paroled for Total 0%–7% and Total 8% plus: χ^2 = 0.637, 1df, p < 0.425, not significant.

Four conclusions can safely be drawn from the data presented in these tables:

- There is a strong and statistically significant correlation between actuarial RORS and the parole decision so far as non-sex offenders were concerned. In other words, whether members of the Board realise it or not, their release decisions reflected in a systematic way statistical risk of reconviction. However, there is no such correlation for sex offenders.

- For non-sex offenders only eight per cent of prisoners with a RORS of 17 per cent or more were released, compared with 83 per cent of those with a RORS of 2 per cent or lower.

- Half of the non-sex offenders had a RORS of 7 per cent or less (an average risk of 3.7%). Forty per cent of this group was denied parole. Thus, as regards risk of reconviction, the Board acted with considerable caution in these cases.

- It was even more cautious as regards sex offenders where only 22 per cent of those with a RORS of 7 per cent or less (average 3.2%) were paroled, not much higher than the 15 per cent paroled where the RORS was 8 per cent or higher.

We also studied the *type* of risk and the *period* during which a reconviction might occur. If the Board were following the Secretary of State's directions, one would expect it to be more concerned about the risk of conviction for a *serious* offence during the parole period, than conviction for any offence (including those which would not result in a further sentence of imprisonment). Similarly, because the Board is directed to take into account *primarily the period when the prisoner would otherwise be in custody*, a higher parole rate would be expected when the same level of risk relates to the longer period of two years from the date of parole eligibility.

This predicted pattern was observed for non-sex offenders. As expected, the proportion of prisoners in the lowest risk category was smallest when it related to any offence over a *period of two years*, and a higher proportion of them was paroled:

	Percentage in 0%–7% risk band	Percentage paroled
● For a serious offence on parole	48%	60%
● For a serious offence over two years	28%	68%
● For any offence on parole	18%	75%
● For any offence over two years	6%	77%

However, this pattern of parole decisions was not observed for sex offenders:

	Percentage in 0%–7% risk band	Percentage paroled
● For a serious offence on parole	64%	22%
● For a serious offence over two years	40%	16%
● For any offence on parole	44%	20%
● For any offence over two years	28%	19%

This means, of course, that the Board appears to be operating a policy, under the directions, which retains in custody four out of five of those long-term sex offenders whose actuarial risk of reconviction for *any offence over a period of two years* lies between zero and 7 per cent.

All of these findings indicate that the Parole Board does not put the same weight on the factors which are reflected in the actuarial ROR when it comes to dealing with sex offenders as it does when deciding whether to parole non-sex offenders. It was therefore decided, first to compare the relationship between such factors and release decisions for non-sex and sex offenders, and secondly to relate parole decisions for sex offenders to a specially devised 'sex-offender prediction tool'.

Factors associated with the parole decision

Table 4.4 shows the parole rate for non-sex and sex offenders in relation to factors which, given the Secretary of State's directions, the Board might be expected to take into account in judging a prisoner's risk and efforts to address offending behaviour.

Table 4.4: **Factors associated with the granting of parole: comparing non-sex offenders with sex offenders[65]**

Factors	Non-sex offenders N = 345		Sex offenders N = 92	
	Percentage paroled	Average RORS	Percentage paroled	Average RORS
Criminal history factors				
No previous convictions	82.9	2.7	25.0	3.5
11 or more previous convictions	14.5	21.1	5.9*	19.8
No previous sex and/or violent conviction	57.5	6.2	21.2	5.7
Sex and/or violent previous conviction	22.6	15.8	17.5	9.9
No previous youth custody	55.2	5.0	21.1	4.8
2 or more previous youth custody	14.7	23.9	0.0*	23.9
No previous adult custody	50.8	6.9	25.8	5.3
5 or more adult custody	5.0	28.6	0.0*	27.0
No previous breach	53.0	6.5	20.8	5.2
Previous supervision and/or bail breach	12.7	18.3	25.0*	29.5
Prison progress factors				
Category D	70.7	7.5	100*	7.3
Category B	8.6	17.2	5.0	7.6
No adjudications	74.7	7.7	19.6	5.7
4 or more adjudications	15.2	14.2	0.0*	11.8
Completed courses in SPO report	56.3	9.6	46.2*	7.5
Not completed courses in SPO report	25.7	13.1	16.0	7.6
Does not deny offence	37.1	12.1	29.1	8.3
Denies offence	41.2*	6.0	5.4	6.5

* These percentages should be treated with caution. They are based on numbers of less than 20.

Five main conclusions emerged:

● Criminal history factors were highly associated with both the average RORS and the parole rate for those convicted of non-sex offences.

---

65   A full list of factors related to the parole rate can be found in Appendix 2.

- Factors associated with a less serious criminal history (especially no previous convictions) were given far less weight for sex offenders than for non-sex offenders. For sex offenders the parole rate was low whatever their previous history.

- Having no prison adjudications was associated with a high parole rate for non-sex offenders but not for sex offenders.

- Both non-sex offenders and sex offenders who had completed all the offending behaviour courses mentioned in the seconded probation officer's report were much more often paroled than were those who had not completed *all* the courses.

- Sex offenders who denied the offence were very rarely paroled, despite the fact that their average RORS was no higher than that of non-sex offender deniers, a much higher proportion of whom were granted parole.

Risk and sex offenders

There were 92 parole applicants who had been convicted of a sexual offence, of whom 18 (19.6%) were released: a similar rate whether they were at their last review or an earlier review. This is a considerably lower parole rate than in 1990 when 30 per cent of sex offenders serving sentences of four years or more who were reviewed during that year were released.[66]

The decline in the use of parole for sex offenders is no doubt in part due to the fact that all prisoners are now supervised after release, whether granted parole or not, whereas in 1990 some may have been released early purely to ensure that they were supervised on parole instead of released 'cold' after serving two-thirds of their sentence. It also reflects the impact of the Secretary of State's directions, which draw attention to the seriousness of the risk of sexual reoffending. Moreover, in interpreting these directions, it would be remarkable if the judgements of Board members were not affected by the substantially increased press and public concern about the risk posed by serious sexual offenders.

As already shown, the prisoner's actuarial RORS was not in the case of sex offenders a major factor explaining who did and who did not get parole. In fact, what mattered was whether the offender admitted or denied his or her guilt, had or had not completed a sex offender treatment programme (known as SOTP), and was considered suitable or unsuitable for parole by the home probation officer. Thus, 40 per cent (37/92) of the sex offenders in the sample had denied their offence and all but two (neither of whom in fact had done SOTP) were refused parole − despite the fact that 17 (46%) of them had a risk of reconviction of committing a serious offence on parole of 2 per cent or less. This contrasts

---

66   Parole Board (1991), Table 2, p. 25. Subsequent reports show a decline in the parole rate for sex offenders.

markedly with the situation under the old parole system. In the study of parole decisions in 1993-94, it was found that two-thirds of the sex offender deniers were paroled at their last review in order to ensure some supervision after release.[66]

Only five of the 56 prisoners (9%) who had not done SOTP were granted parole. For a variety of reasons all of them were regarded as very low risks. But completing a SOTP course was not in itself sufficient: the panel had to be satisfied that real progress had been made in addressing the sexual problems which were thought to put the offender at risk of committing further sexual offences. The Board believed that only 14 of the 36 (39%) who had completed SOTP during their current sentence had reduced their risk sufficiently to warrant parole (although one was refused because of an unsatisfactory release plan). Of the 13 paroled, 12 were required to undertake further work on their sexual offending while on licence.

It mattered enormously whether a sex offender was recommended by his or her home probation officer. Seventy per cent were not and only one of them was paroled. In contrast, 61 per cent of the HPOs' positive recommendations were accepted by the Board.

The lack of a strong association between the actuarial RORS and the Board's decisions in relation to sex offenders is probably due to the fact that Board members considered that many sex offenders posed a relatively high risk whatever their official criminal histories might have been. No doubt they were aware that behind a conviction for some types of sexual crime might lie a lengthy, previously undisclosed, involvement in sexual deviance. This is probably why so great an emphasis was placed on acceptance of guilt and involvement in programmes specially designed to challenge sexual fantasies and presumptions associated with inappropriate sexual conduct.

Psychologists who specialise in sexual deviance have turned their attention to the distinctive problem of assessing the risk posed by sexual offenders. In relation to parole, members of the Board have been informed about the development of a prediction instrument based on research by Dr David Thornton of HM Prison Service. According to this instrument – called *A Simple Actuarial Risk Classification Procedure for Assessing Long Term Risk of Sex Offenders* – five main factors, and several further aggravating factors, are associated with three risk levels of reconviction for a violent or sexual offence over a period of two (and also of ten) years.[67] However, it does not provide an estimate of the risk during the shorter parole period when the offender would otherwise be in custody. Nevertheless, it is reasonable to assume that about 60 per cent of those who would be reconvicted in a two-year follow-up

---

66   It is interesting to note that in that study it was also found that at least 35 per cent of the 126 sex offenders were deniers. See Hood and Shute, (1995), para. 57 and fn. 79.

67   One point is given for each of the following features: 1. 'The index offence includes a sexual offence'; 2. 'Index conviction includes non-sexual violence as a separate charge'; 3. 'Previous convictions include a sexual offence'; 4. 'Previous convictions include non-sexual violence'; 5. 'Convicted on more than three occasions prior to the index conviction'. One point places the prisoner in Level I; 2 to 3 points in Level II; 4 or more points in Level III. In addition, 'where more information is available it is possible to refine the initial classification a little' by taking into account seven 'additional factors [which] have consistently emerged as predictors'. They are: male victims under the age of 16; range of offending, especially stranger victims; non-contact sex offences in the record; problematic substance abuse; psychopathy as defined by the Hare PCL; never married or lived in long-term relationships; deviant arousal as measured by PPG. The possession of two of these 'aggravating circumstances' raises the risk to the next Level.

period would be convicted during an eight to12 months parole licence period (assuming that the parole licence itself does not suppress still further the propensity to commit crime).[68]

Sex offenders in Level I have a 2 per cent predicted risk over two years of a reconviction for a sexual or violent offence. Those in Level II have a predicted 15 per cent risk. And those in Level III a 36 per cent predicted risk.[69] The risk within each Level is reduced by 40 per cent if the offender has completed a SOTP course.[70] According to the information provided to members of the Board by Dr Thornton, 'Level III cases pose a significant risk even in the short term' while 'Level II and even perhaps Level I cases pose a significant long term risk'.

It was not known what use Parole Board members made of their knowledge of this methodology for assessing risk. The researchers certainly heard nothing during observations of panel discussions to indicate that it was widely used. However, it was possible to calculate the extent to which parole decisions reflected the risk as defined by the Thornton scale (see Table 4.5). This takes into account, where the information was available in the dossier, both aggravating factors and reports on the prisoner's response to SOTP.

Table 4.5: Number and percentage of sex offenders falling into sex offender risk bands (taking into account aggravating factors and SOTP completion*) by percentage released and SOTP completion

Two-year risk level	Number and percentage in risk level	SOTP completed yes or no	Predicted two-year reconviction rate for a sexual or violent crime	Number in each predicted band	Number released in each predicted band	Percentage released
I	31 (33.7%)	Yes	1%	13 (4)	4 (4)	30.8 {29.0
		No	2%	18	5	27.8
II	36 (39.1%)	Yes	9%	13 (5)	4 (4)	30.8 {11.1
		No	15%	23	0	0.0
III	25 (27.2%)	Yes	22%	10 (5)	5 (5)	50.0 {20.0
		No	36%	15	0	0.0
Total	92			92	18 (13)	19.6

*   The bracketed figures in columns 5 and 6 refer to those cases where the panel judged risk to have been sufficiently reduced by SOTP to warrant parole.

68   This has been calculated by comparing for our sample of sex offenders the ROR for a serious offence during the parole period with the ROR for a serious offence over two years. A similar ratio has been found by follow-up studies. See, for example, Lloyd, Mair and Hough (1994), p 45, which found that of all offenders (i.e. including non-prisoners) who were reconvicted within two years, 'the majority (69%) received their first conviction within a year of sentence/discharge'.
69   The ten-year predicted risks are: Level I, 13%; Level II, 38%; Level III, 66%.
70   A comparison was made between the risk as predicted by the RORS and the risk as predicted by the 'Thornton scale'. This showed that the Thornton scale discriminated between the RORS scores for sex offenders: the average RORS for Thornton Level I was 6.2%; for Level II, 12.1%; and Level III, 19.3%. In relation to individuals, about half the 92 sex offenders had similar scores on both scales. But a quarter were rated as a considerably higher risk by the Thornton score than by the RORS, and a quarter were rated as a less serious risk by the sex-offender predictor than by the RORS.

The following conclusions stand out:

- A third of the sex offenders were in Level I. They posed a very low risk of being reconvicted for a violent or sexual offence over two years, and obviously an even lower risk during a shorter possible parole period. Nevertheless, the Board was cautious, releasing less than a third of them, whether or not they had completed SOTP.

- Four out of ten were in Level II, for whom the risk of being convicted of a further sexual or violent offence over two years was between 9 per cent and 15 per cent. Nine out of ten of them were refused parole. Those released were all judged by the panel to have had the risk they posed reduced by successful completion of SOTP.

- Just over a quarter were placed in Level III, the highest risk band. Five (20%) were released, all of whom the panel judged to have successfully completed SOTP.

- The statistical risk of reconviction according to the Thornton scale is a less strong predictor of release than whether the prisoner had successfully completed SOTP. Of those who had done so, the proportion paroled was virtually the same whatever the Thornton risk category of the prisoner had been.

It is therefore clear that what is regarded by many as a more appropriate risk prediction instrument for sex offenders than the 'general ROR' does not, by itself, explain the low rate of parole granted to sex offenders as a category.

'Clinical' assessments of risk compared with actuarial risk

As explained above, panel members no longer have available to them the actuarial ROR. They therefore have to make risk assessments on the basis of their general reading of the dossier. It has been shown that they take into account many of the factors that are summarised in the actuarial ROR – especially number of previous convictions and previous custodial sentences – as well as factors highly correlated with previous convictions, such as the number of previous failures on supervision. But were panel members' *'clinical' estimates* of the risk posed by individual prisoners concordant with the *actuarial risks* for those prisoners, as statistically calculated from the follow-up records of a large number of prisoners?

Thus, each panel member was asked to complete six 'risk assessments' for each prisoner under consideration (risk of conviction for a *serious* offence and for *any* offence during the parole period, over two years *if granted* parole, and over two years *if not granted* parole).

For each risk assessment they were asked to choose an appropriate risk band: 'low' (between 0% and 19%), 'moderate' (between 20% and 39%), about '50/50' (between 40% and 59%), 'high' (between 60% and 79%) or 'very high' (80% and higher). Within the band chosen they were invited to indicate, if they could, a precise percentage risk of reconviction or, if unable to do so, to tick the appropriate risk band. The vast majority of panel members did the latter.

The following comparisons emerged:

● Only 15 per cent of prisoners in our sample had an actuarial ROR of a *serious* offence during the parole period of 20 per cent or higher, yet lead panel members considered that 59 per cent posed that level of risk.

● Lead members estimated that 22 per cent of the prisoners had a 60 per cent or higher risk of being reconvicted for any offence while on parole. In fact, only three per cent had such a high risk.

● At the other end of the scale, 59 per cent had a 'low' (19% or less) actuarial ROR for any offence during the period of the parole licence, but lead members thought that only 35 per cent of the prisoners had such a low-risk.

A similar pattern emerged when a comparison was made for sex offenders between lead members' assessments of risk and the Thornton sex offender prediction instrument. As shown above in Table 4.5, 73 per cent of the cases fell into Levels I and II (broadly equivalent to a risk of reconviction for a *sexual or violent offence* of less than 20% over two years). Yet lead members estimated that less than half the sex offenders had a risk of being convicted for a serious offence *of any kind* over two years of less than 20 per cent.

Thus, this study has found strong evidence that panel members were making decisions, in aggregate, on the basis of unduly pessimistic 'clinical' estimations of risk when compared with actuarial calculations of risk.

The same was broadly true of home and seconded probation officers. In a similar proportion of cases they also gave higher predictions of risk than the actuarial calculation would suggest.[71] However, when the 'clinical' assessments of risk made by seconded and home probation officers were compared with those of lead members, the degree of concordance between their assessments was not high. Only half the home probation officers and 38 per cent of the seconded probation officers estimated the RORS to be in the same broad risk band as the lead member. Indeed, just 30 per cent of prisoners were placed in the same RORS band by all three assessors.[72]

---

71   For example, with regard to the tracked prisoners, only 16 per cent had an actuarial RORS of 20 per cent or higher. Yet, HPOs estimated that 58 per cent, SPOs 60 per cent, and Lead members 63 per cent of the tracked prisoners they assessed had a RORS of 20 per cent or higher.

72   These comparisons could only be made, of course, for those tracked cases for which a RORS assessment had been made by the SPO, HPO and lead panel member.

An attempt was made to assess the extent to which lead members believed that if they granted parole it would reduce the risk of reconviction for a serious offence over a two-year period. This was done by comparing their assessments of risk 'if the prisoner were granted parole' with their assessments of risk 'if not granted parole'. Table 4.6 shows how many thought the risk would be reduced, remain the same, or increased if parole were granted.

Table 4.6:   Lead member assessment of risk of reconviction for a serious offence over two years if parole were to be granted and if parole were not granted [73]

Two-year risk if granted parole	Two-year risk if not granted parole					
	Very high	High	50/50	Moderate	Low	Total
Very high	19					19
High	6	49	9			64
50/50		10	58	6		74
Moderate		1	17	71		89
Low				15	105	120
Total	25	60	84	92	105	366

Non-shaded areas indicate the lead member thinks the risk will be the same whether or not the prisoner is granted parole

When the above assessments by lead members were related to the decision whether or not to grant parole, the following finding emerged:

- For 302 prisoners (83%) lead members chose the same risk band, whether parole was to be granted or not. It can be inferred from this that most lead members did not believe that by granting parole the risk would be substantially reduced. [74]

Lead members' assessments were compared with those of home probation officers who judged that for a quarter (27%) of the prisoners the risk of reconviction of a serious offence would be reduced over a two-year period if they were to be granted parole: twice as many as lead members estimated. [75] It can be reasonably inferred that home probation officers were considerably more optimistic about the effectiveness of parole in reducing risk than were Parole Board members – a finding that needs to be borne in mind when interpreting the response of the Parole Board to probation officers' recommendations, discussed in Chapter 5.

---

73   These calculations were also made for Lead members' assessments of the risk of a conviction for any offence over a two-year period. The findings were almost identical.

74   That is, sufficient to move the prisoner from one broad risk band to another. Parole was in fact granted most often in those cases where the lead members had judged the risk to be low irrespective of whether parole would be granted: in 78 per cent of the 105 cases.

75   But SPOs were more like lead members in this respect. They judged that risk would be reduced by parole for 15 per cent of prisoners.

The need for actuarial risk assessments

Underestimation of risk?

It might be argued that the Risk of Reconviction scores underestimated the true actuarial risk of reconviction posed by the sample of prisoners in this study. However, there is good reason to believe that this was not the case. Their average expected rate of reconviction within two years for a serious offence (defined as one which would be likely to lead to imprisonment) was 17.8 per cent. This is very similar, bearing in mind the nature of the sample of cases observed in this study,[76] to the national figures. These show that, of all prisoners who had served a determinate sentence of four years or longer who were released from custody in 1995, 15.5 per cent were sentenced to a further term of imprisonment on their first reconviction within two years of their discharge.

However, both the ROR and Thornton prediction tools appear to have overestimated the likely reconviction rate of the sex offenders. The national follow-up figures show that, of all sex offenders discharged from a prison sentence of four or more years in 1995, only six per cent were reconvicted and sentenced to imprisonment on their first reconviction over a follow-up period of two years. And only 2.7 per cent were reconvicted and imprisoned on their first reconviction of a sexual (1.3 %) or violent (1.4 %) offence.[77]

Yet the ROR predicted that 12 per cent of the 92 sex offenders in the sample would be reconvicted of a serious offence likely to lead to imprisonment within two years and the Thornton Scale predicted that nearly 14 per cent would be reconvicted of a sexual or violent offence within two years: four times as many as the national follow-up statistics show.

Thus, in aggregate, the estimates made by Parole Board members, for the purposes of this research, of the likelihood of sex offenders being reconvicted of a serious offence within two years, look rather more pessimistic when compared with the national follow-up statistics than they did when compared with the ROR or Thornton scores.

The ROR as a guide to decision-making

Since the primary concern of the Parole Board is to make decisions based on risk, it is essential for the protection of the public and for the just treatment of prisoners – who should not remain in custody on false assumptions of their risk – that actuarial risk assessments be made available in every case to guide Parole Board members' decisions. The ROR calculated by Professor Copas and his colleagues now should be brought up-to-date to see whether the inclusion of 'dynamic variables', relating to the prisoner's behaviour and

---

76   It is likely that our sample was biased somewhat towards a higher proportion of high-risk prisoners, for the proportion of them paroled was slightly below the average.
77   These figures were especially calculated for us by Stephen White of the Home Office Research, Development and Statistics Directorate from the data reported in Kershaw, Goodman and White (1999). The figures were recalculated to show reconvictions by type of original offence and type of offence on first reconviction for all prisoners discharged from determinate sentences of four years or longer.

response to 'offending-behaviour' programmes in custody, aids in the prediction of reoffending. In addition, further efforts should be made to build on the experience of developing risk assessments for special categories of prisoner, particularly sexual and violent offenders. To make all this possible it will be necessary to improve the way in which assessments of prisoners' responses to offending behaviour programmes are recorded in parole dossiers. For example, it was noted that it was often difficult to judge whether a 'treatment programme' had been successfully completed and, if it has, whether its completion was considered to have lowered the risk of reconviction. However, some Sex Offender Treatment Programme reports included a standard form on which risk was rated both at the commencement and termination of the course. We recommend that this good practice should be followed consistently, not only for SOTP, but also for all types of offending-behaviour programmes as they become accredited and the research evidence on their effectiveness accumulates. As well as possibly improving actuarial risk prediction, such assessments should assist Board members in dealing with individual cases to follow directions that require them to assess, in relation to risk, the prisoner's 'progress' in addressing his or her offending behaviour.

Chapter 5   The role of probation officers' reports

To what extent were probation officers' recommendations followed?

It is hardly surprising to find that both seconded and home probation officers had a major influence on parole decisions. With the exception of psychiatrists, who report on a few prisoners, they are now the only participants in the system that make recommendations to the Board.[78]

Interviews with seconded probation officers, and the questionnaire sent to home probation officers, revealed that they tried to make clear-cut recommendations to the Board – YES or NO – wherever possible, and indeed they did so in about 85 per cent of the 438 cases in this study. Not all the officers felt able to estimate how often their recommendations were followed.[79] But most of those who were able to do so said that if they made a negative recommendation the Board would almost certainly follow it. On the other hand, a positive recommendation was likely to be followed in only about half the cases. Table 5.1 shows how right they were. This is probably why a quarter of both seconded and home probation officers said they disagreed 'quite often' with the reasons for refusal given by the Board. Indeed, as many as one-third of the seconded probation officers said that, in their view, the Board failed to select accurately prisoners who 'will keep out of trouble while on licence and benefit from parole'.

Table 5.1 also shows that:

- When both probation officers recommended parole, the proportion of prisoners paroled was 54 per cent, 60 per cent higher than the average rate of 34 per cent.

- When only one probation officer recommended parole, only 18 per cent were granted it.

- When neither probation officer was willing to support the application, the proportion granted parole was tiny: 2.3 per cent.

Overall, four out of 10 prisoners refused parole by the Board had been recommended for it by probation officers. If the Parole Board had released all the prisoners who both probation officers had recommended as suitable, the release rate *for the sample as a whole* would have been not 33.6 per cent but 59.6 per cent: 77 per cent higher.

---

78   Under the 'old' parole system, form LB2 contained a recommendation from an Assistant Governor. In a major study of parole decisions, Nuttall *et al.* (1977), p. 38, found that Local Review Committees followed Assistant Governors' recommendations in 86 per cent of cases.

79   One-third of the SPOs, but 60 per cent of the HPOs, indicated that they systematically monitored Parole Board decisions relating to prisoners for whom they had prepared a report.

Table 5.1: The relationship between probation officers' recommendations and parole decisions

Recommendation	Number	Percentage of total	Number paroled	Percentage paroled
Both SPO and HPO YES	247	56.4	133	53.8
Only one YES*	60	13.7	11	18.3
Neither YES**	131	29.9	3	2.3
Total	438	100	147	33.6

*   In 27 (45%) of these cases the other probation officer said NO and in the remaining 33 cases the other probation officer either made no recommendation or submitted no report.

**   In 92 of these 131 cases (70%) both probation officers recommended NO. In 20, one of the two probation officers recommended NO and in the remaining 19 cases the probation officers either made no recommendation or did not submit a report. All three cases where the panel released the prisoner despite neither probation officer recommending parole had very low actuarial RORSs of 5 per cent or less. In only one of these cases did both probation officers recommend NO; in the other two, one of the officers made no recommendation.

The Board was wary of going against probation officers' negative recommendations. This is probably because, if they were to do so and the prisoner were to commit a very serious offence while on parole, it would be hard to explain publicly why the advice of the persons who had interviewed the prisoner and knew the home circumstances had not been followed. But why did the Board reject almost half the prisoners who had been recommended for release by both their inside and outside probation officers?

Probation officers' recommendations in relation to ROR

In order to shed light on this question, an analysis was made of the cases where both the SPO and HPO recommended parole but the Parole Board refused to grant it, taking into account actuarial prediction of risk of reconviction. Table 5.2 shows clearly that the Board was much more likely to agree with the probation officers' recommendation when the actuarial risk of reconviction for a serious offence during parole was low:

- When the RORS was between zero and 7 per cent, 71 per cent of recommended prisoners were paroled.

- When the RORS was 8 per cent or higher, only 30 per cent of recommended prisoners were paroled.[80]

---

80   The parole rate for recommended sex offenders with a RORS of 7 per cent or less was 66.6 per cent, and for non-sex offenders was 71.3 per cent. For those with a RORS of 8 per cent or more, 28 per cent of non-sex offenders were released compared to 50 per cent of ten sex offenders. The numbers are small and the differences not statistically significant.

Table 5.2: SPO and HPO recommend parole (n = 246*): parole rates in relation to ROR for a serious offence on parole licence

Actuarial ROR	Number and percentage in each risk band		Number and percentage granted parole	
Serious offence while on parole	Number	Percentage	Number	Percentage
0%–2%	50	20.3	44	88.0
3%–4%	50	20.3	28	56.0
5%–7%	44	17.9	30	68.2
Total 0%–7%	144	58.5	102	70.8
8%–10%	34	13.8	12	35.3
11%–16%	36	14.6	13	36.1
17% and higher	32	13.0	6	18.8
Total 8% and higher	102	41.5	31	30.4
Total	246	100	133	54.1

$\chi2 = 52.35$, 5df, p<.0001 * The ROR could not be calculated for one case.

Table 5.3 reveals a similar pattern in relation to the ROR for *any* offence during the parole licence. A quarter of the prisoners had a probability of being convicted of *any* offence during the parole licence period of 7 per cent or below (on average 4.5%), yet a quarter of them were rejected by the Board.

Table 5.3: SPO and HPO recommend parole (n = 246*): parole rates in relation to ROR for any offence on parole licence

Actuarial ROR	Number and percentage in each risk band		Number and percentage granted parole	
Any offence while on parole	Number	Percentage	Number	Percentage
0%–2%	12	4.9	10	83.3
3%–4%	22	8.9	18	81.8
5%–7%	31	12.6	21	67.7
Total 0%–7%	65	26.4	49	75.4
8%–10%	30	12.2	21	70.0
11%–16%	41	16.7	24	58.5
17% and higher	110	44.7	39	35.5
Total 8% and higher	181	73.6	84	46.4
Total	246	100	133	54.1

$\chi2 = 32.03$, 5df, p<.0001 * The ROR could not be calculated for one case.

To what extent was the difference of opinion between the probation officers and Parole Board members on prisoners' suitability for parole due to differences in the estimates they made of the risk of reconviction? Table 5.4 shows, for those cases recommended by both probation officers, the association between lead members' 'clinical' estimates of risk and parole decisions. As one might expect, panels rejected a high proportion (81%) of prisoners who they assumed presented quite a high risk (20% or higher) of being convicted of a serious offence while on parole. Nevertheless, one in five of those judged to be a high risk were released with both probation officers' support, and a similar proportion of those judged to pose a 'low-risk' were refused, despite the favourable recommendations.

What is particularly striking is that lead members estimated the risk of reconviction for a serious offence on parole licence to be 20 per cent or higher for 43 per cent of the prisoners who had been recommended for parole by both probation officers. In fact, the actuarial RORS was this high for only one in ten of them. This is another indicator that Board members could be helped in making decisions if they had available to them an actuarially-based risk of reconviction score.

Table 5.4: SPO and HPO recommend parole: the relationship between lead panel members' estimates of ROR of a serious offence on parole licence and parole decisions (n = 208*)

Lead members' estimate	Number of cases estimated by lead members in risk bands	Percentage of lead members' estimates in risk bands	Percentage of cases in actuarial ROR risk bands	Parole Board granted parole	
				No.	%
Low (0%–19%)	118	56.7	89.9	96	81.4
20% and higher	90	43.3	10.1	17	18.9
Total	208			113	54.3

$\chi2 = 80.295$, 1df, p< .0001 *In 38 cases the lead member had not made this estimate.

These findings reflect a marked difference of view in general between probation officers and Board members in relation to the risk they felt it right to take when recommending or granting parole. Indeed, taking into account all 438 cases in the sample:

● Where the seconded and home probation officers estimated the risk of reconviction for a serious offence while on parole to be 20 per cent or higher they recommended release for 44 and 51 per cent of prisoners respectively.

● However, panels agreed to grant parole in only nine per cent of cases where the lead member estimated that risk to be 20 per cent or higher.

This is consistent with the hypothesis that probation officers believe more often than do Parole Board members that public protection can be better served by releasing a prisoner earlier in the sentence so that he/she can benefit from the longer period of supervision which a parole licence provides, rather than by continued imprisonment followed by a shorter period on licence.

When actuarial risk is low yet parole is denied

Why did the panels refuse parole in the 42 cases where both probation officers had recommended release and the RORS was 7 per cent or less? The first thing to note is that these cases were more likely to generate disagreement amongst panel members than was usual.[81] Furthermore, even when two members were somewhat in favour, a strong negative opinion could decide the issue. For example:

Case 297 was serving four years for robbery having had his application for parole deferred from a previous panel to obtain a report on his cognitive skills course. The lead member rated him a '50/50' risk for both a serious offence and for any offence, although the other two members considered him a 'low' risk. The actuarial RORS for a serious offence while on parole was 4 per cent, and for any offence 10 per cent:

Independent member (lead): *At the time of the PBIM interview he was attending a cognitive skills course ... I rang the prison and asked for the relevant documents. The prisoner's concern seems to be over the deprivation he suffers from being in prison, in other words being away from his family, which seems to override any concern he has for the victim. There is nothing in here that makes me ready to release.* Second Independent member: *I had him as an iffy. He is still quite young and he is quite immature. I could well go with a no.* Third Independent member: *I went the other way ... My impression is that he tried very hard and there is confirmation that he is growing in maturity ... I was prepared to give him a chance. You're iffy and one other clearly NO. I am in a minority and I don't want to dig my heels in.*

Reasons: *He is serving his first custodial sentence having committed a robbery which, although no weapons were used, was particularly threatening in nature and would have caused the victims considerable trauma ... Although he has taken part in some offence-focused work from which he is said to have gained a degree of benefit, more needs to be done to enable him to develop a deeper insight into his offending so that he really appreciates the effect that his behaviour has on others. Until this is done, the panel considers that the risk to the public is too high for early release on parole licence to be granted.*

The overwhelming reason why panels did not grant parole – mentioned in 40 of the 42 cases – was that the prisoner had not, in their view, made sufficient progress in addressing

---

81   In 14/42 cases (33%) compared with 59/396 (15%) in the remainder of the observed sample.

his or her offending behaviour.[82] In half of these cases (19/40) the panel said that the prisoner should stay in custody in order 'to do further work', despite the fact that both probation officers felt either that enough work on offending behaviour had already been done, or that it could be completed satisfactorily in the community. The following case is an interesting example:

Case 90, serving eight years for drug importation. It was his first review. The lead member 'clinically' assessed the RORS as 'moderate' (20%–39%) and the RORA as '50/50' (40%–59%). The actuarial RORS was 3 per cent, and RORA 6 per cent:

Independent member (lead): *He's a man in his 50s. He's in cat D … We're looking here at 15 months on parole which is a long time … I'm saying NO, he has another review.* Second independent member: *Both probation officers are supporting him. His prison record is good. He needs to do a little more work perhaps.* Lead: *But the inside probation officer says he's a risk.* Third Independent member: *I am concerned about the serious escalation of offending. He went back to offending very quickly this time.* Lead: *He admits he's a greedy man. Not this time.*

Reasons: … *Prison behaviour has been excellent and there are signs that thinking has been changing. However, the panel concludes that greater insight and understanding into the causes and consequences of behaviour needs to be acquired through more intensely focused work, thereby providing some assurance that the risk of reoffending has been reduced.*

Why had both probation officers recommended parole?

The SPO's report was very supportive. She wrote: *He appears to have benefited fully from all offence-focused work … He successfully applied for the resettlement scheme … and is currently working for a building firm as an estimator … He has used his time in prison constructively and made every attempt to change his thinking and thus change his behaviour accordingly … [He] is unlikely to repeat further mistakes. There is little to be gained by further time in custody.*

The HPO wrote: *He has attended courses within the prison and his participation has led to greater insight into the wider effects of his criminal behaviour … He appears motivated towards refraining from further offending and settling down with his partner in the family home. Moreover, he has demonstrated in the past and during this prison sentence that he is able to comply with supervision in the community.*

In those cases where 'further work' on offending behaviour *in prison* was *not* given as the reason for refusal, the issue usually came down to whether to trust the prisoner or not. For example:

---

82   The other two cases were refused largely because of an inadequate release plan. Of the 40 prisoners who had not completed offending behaviour work in prison, five had also committed a breach of trust. But for three of them the positive probation reports had been written after this had happened. In analysing the dossiers it was also found that the 42 who were refused had an average of 4.8 adjudications for prison offences recorded against them, compared with an average of 1.4 for the 102 low-risk recommended prisoners who were released.

Case 59. This 26-year-old prisoner was serving five years for robbery. He had eight previous convictions but it was his first prison sentence. All three members placed the RORS in the 'moderate' (20%–39%) risk category. For any offence (RORA), the lead and one other member indicated the risk was 'moderate' and the third member that it was '50/50'. The actuarial RORS was 7 per cent, and RORA 17 per cent. The prisoner in his written representations, after reading the report of his interview with the PBIM, wrote: *I really hope that all the positive work I have put in to change my life will be of some help to my chances.*

Independent member (lead): *As a result of the 1998 drugs offences in prison, the probation officer got to work on drug behaviour. He's done a drugs course, education. He's got a college place. All support him — educational course and drugs and OB. I said YES.* Second Independent member: *I said NO ... Look at the previous convictions. He failed a MDT in April. His ETS marks are not very good. His heroin addiction causes problems. He has a two-year probation order for violence and then went out and committed an offence of violence.* Third Independent member: *I am impressed he's been offered a college place. He is a risk but on the positive side he's worked hard to put the past behind him and the probation officer is also behind him.* Second IM: *With the violence in his past I don't feel he's done enough. He is a recidivist.* Lead: *My head says NO, but my heart says maybe ... When one looks at the risk factors the case for release could not be substantiated.*

In concluding its **Reasons** the panel *noted his record of offending and breaches of trust and consider that he poses too high a risk for release on parole.*

Why had both probation officers recommended parole?

The SPO wrote: *Whereas it is unwise to be over-optimistic where drug addiction is concerned, it is seldom that I have met an inmate who has shown the strength and determination to remain drug free, and is aware of the pitfalls he may encounter.* The HPO wrote: *I have noted considerable and positive changes in his attitude and his ability to rationalise his past and current behaviour ... In my view the chances of his becoming involved in such an offence again is small. With appropriate support in avoiding the use of drugs the chances of him reoffending will be further reduced ... The effort he has already displayed during his time served in custody is, I believe, a measure of his remorse and willingness to make amends ... He is at a stage in his life when he is less likely to offend than at any other time since I have known him.*

Thus, the reason these 42 low-risk prisoners were refused appears again to be linked to 'clinical' judgements about the level of risk that they posed. Indeed, in eight out of ten of these cases lead members had estimated the risk of reconviction for a serious offence while on parole to be 20 per cent or higher: considerably in excess of the actuarial risk. Once more this suggests that Board members would be assisted in their task if they were able to compare their 'clinical' predictions with an actuarial prediction score.

High-risk prisoners recommended for parole

Table 5.1 showed that more than 40 per cent of the prisoners for whom both probation officers recommended parole had an actuarial ROR for a serious offence while on parole licence of 8 per cent or above. The Board refused 70 per cent of them. Nevertheless, nearly one in five of those with the highest actuarial RORS (17% or higher) were paroled. Such prisoners were regarded as 'truly changed men', the exemplars of what could be achieved by making the best of the opportunities available for doing courses and improving educational and employment skills. An example was:

Case 373 who was serving eight years. It was his second and last review. The lead member rated risk of reconviction for both a serious offence and any offence while on parole licence as 'low' (0%–19%). The actuarial ROR for a serious offence was 49 per cent, and for any offence 74 per cent.

Independent member (lead): *This is a 33-year-old … He would be on parole for six months. The eight years were made up of two four-year sentences for burglary. While he was serving the first sentence he went on a town visit, failed to return and committed two other burglaries. He said he had a row with his girlfriend, so 'sensibly didn't return to prison'. I found this surprising, and I surprised myself on balance, by saying YES.* Second Independent member: *I have him as a NO.* Lead: *OK, I will go through the details. He had been in care … He has a number of previous convictions but very little violence. Quite a lot of breach of court orders … He … drifted into crime … At the last review, he was turned down but since then he has done well. He has been well behaved. He is in Category C on enhanced regime. He has had a credit given to him for giving evidence against [an offender]. He's done courses. Everyone is in favour of parole in the reports and he has a job offer. The seconded probation officer says that he sees real change, real maturation, and that he would do well on supervision. He has only got until September, and I thought, let's go for it.* Second Independent: *But he committed offences when at large. The last panel expected him to do offending behaviour courses. The work he has done appears to be anger control and a drug project.* Lead: *He's done OB before and repeated it.* Probation member: *I was a NO myself, but he's been on the list for advanced ETS, but he hasn't done it through no fault of his.* Second Independent: *The prison probation officer says he's the lowest risk he has ever been. He's got six months, in reality four months, left. I think there is a scintilla of risk, but I'll give him the benefit of the doubt.* Probation member (chair): *It was good to have this discussed. I was negative but am persuaded that the behaviour in the last few months has been very positive, so we're all convinced.*

Reasons: *He committed two dwelling house burglaries after failing to return from a town visit in 1995. He has a history of burglary, and he previously offended while subject to licence and supervision. This behaviour has made it difficult to trust him. On the other hand, current reports indicate a growing maturity and change of attitude. … In all these circumstances the panel concluded that the risk of reoffending had been reduced to a level where it could be managed in the community, and that he would derive substantial benefit from the slightly longer period on licence.*

On the other hand, those who could not demonstrate such change, even when this was not their fault, found themselves unable to counter the concerns about risk that their past history raised:

Case 352, serving six years for dealing in class A drugs (heroin and cocaine). The lead member correctly estimated the risk of reconviction for a serious offence in line with the actuarial ROR of 25 per cent. (The same was true of the risk of any offence: this was estimated as '50/50' and was in fact 45%.) The discussion and reading of reasons was completed in two minutes.

Full-time Independent member: *This is a clear NO on the grounds of his record.* Second Independent member (who had rated the risk as 'low'): *My heart said YES but my head said NO, and my head has to rule.*

Reasons: *Mr X has a lengthy history of offending, including convictions for violence, prior to the serious index offence. Numerous custodial sentences have failed to deter him in the past. He has behaved well in custody. He has not, however, undertaken any work aimed at reducing his risk of reoffending and his lengthy criminal history indicates that that risk remains too high to justify early release on licence.*

Why had the probation officers recommended parole?

The SPO said he was *optimistic that the risk of further offending would be low.* He said that the prisoner was aware that the Board would be looking for evidence to show that his risk to the public had diminished but that the prisoner had *not been able to demonstrate this for reasons beyond his control.* He noted that the prisoner had unfortunately been unable to obtain places on the courses identified as appropriate to his particular type of offending [drug supply]. The prisoner was currently awaiting assessment for an ETS [Enhanced Thinking Skills] course but this course was *heavily oversubscribed and it may be some time before a place is offered to him ... At present this aspect of his offending could only be adequately addressed through community based supervision.* The SPO said he was mindful of the fact it was his one and only chance of parole and supported his application.

The HPO, who also recommended parole, said that the prisoner had not undertaken any specific offence related work but this was not the prisoner's fault. She added: *I do not feel he should be unduly penalised because of this.* She indicated that she had referred the prisoner to the local probation service 'Pathways to Change Programme', an offending behaviour programme specifically designed for drug dealers. The prisoner had been accepted as a suitable candidate. Both the SPO and HPO recommended that attendance at this course be made a condition of his licence.

What would be the consequence of increasing the paroling rate of recommended low-risk prisoners?

It is obviously a matter for judgement what level of risk should preclude release on parole when the prisoner has been recommended by both probation officers. For example, it might be argued that a much higher proportion (perhaps all) of recommended prisoners with a ROR of 7 per cent or less for a serious offence while on parole licence are worthy of parole. In the sample studied, the average risk of reconviction for a serious offence on parole licence of those low-risk recommended prisoners who *were* paroled (102) was 3.3 per cent. The 42 who were *not* paroled had slightly worse criminal histories: their average RORS was 4.0 per cent. Thus, if all 144 had been paroled, the *average* risk would have risen to 3.5 per cent. In other words, the number expected to be reconvicted of a serious offence on parole licence would have increased from *three* (3.3% of 102) to *five* (3.5% of 144). Looked at another way, 40 'false positive' prisoners were kept in custody to prevent two 'true positives' being reconvicted.[83]

Furthermore, if all these 144 prisoners had been released, the parole rate for *the sample as a whole* would have been ten percentage points higher (43.2% rather than 33.6%) – equivalent to a 28.5 per cent increase in the parole rate. And the effect of releasing these 42 further prisoners, all of whom had a low probability of reconviction, would be to *lower* the *average* predicted failure rate for all released on parole from 6.2 to 5.7 per cent: a reduction of eight per cent.[84]

The sample studied was approximately 7.5 per cent of all cases decided by the Board in 1998-99. Assuming that this sample was reasonably representative, an estimate was made of the number of prisoners per year that might be expected to be in the low-risk band (0%–7%) and be recommended by both probation officers. From this it was calculated[85] that if the Board had released all such prisoners:

- Approximately 550 additional prisoners would have received parole.

- Of these, approximately 4 per cent (say 22) would be predicted to be reconvicted of a serious offence during the parole licence and approximately 10 per cent (say 55) would be predicted to be reconvicted of any offence during the parole period.

- Thus, about 500 would be expected to complete their parole period without a conviction of any kind.

83   Altogether, the average risk of reconviction of any offence for this group while on parole was 8.8 per cent: equivalent to 13 of the 144 prisoners. In order not to appear too precise, this figure has been rounded to 10 per cent in the second bullet point below. The predicted rate of reconviction for a serious offence on parole licence has similarly been rounded from 3.5 per cent to 4 per cent.

84   If these 42 prisoners had been paroled, the total number released on parole in the sample would have been 189. The average RORS of these prisoners was 5.7 per cent, compared with the average RORS of 6.2 per cent of the 147 prisoners who were actually released. Thus, by paroling a higher proportion of the low-risk prisoners, the overall predicted reconviction rate would fall by eight per cent (from 6.2% to 5.7%).

85   5,875 DCR cases were considered by the Board in 1998–99: see Parole Board (1993), p. 44. Applying the percentage in our sample who were 0%–7% RORS and recommended by both probation officers (32.9%), the yearly total of such prisoners could be expected to be 1,933. Of these, 70.8 per cent would (on the basis of this study) be likely to be paroled, leaving about 550 not paroled.

Given the expense of imprisonment as compared to supervision in the community, the cost of not granting parole to so many prisoners is considerable. It might be more constructive if more of them were paroled and the money saved spent on bolstering offending behaviour programmes and providing closer supervision in the community, with the prospect of perhaps reducing the risk to the public even further.

As already mentioned (see page 35 above) the risk of reconviction scores for parole was used in the old parole system for ensuring that relatively low-risk prisoners received consideration by the Board, whether or not they had been recommended for parole by a Local Review Committee. There is thus a precedent for suggesting that the ROR (or an updated version of it) should again be used to ensure that the Board has its attention drawn to cases which have a low actuarial risk of reconviction. It is therefore recommended that consideration should be given to drawing panel members' attention to the need to consider carefully the actuarial prediction of risk of reconviction in cases where both probation officers have recommended release on parole licence.

Chapter 6 Predicting parole decisions

Creating a statistical model

Through the use of logistic regression analysis a prediction model of parole decision-making was calculated. Ten variables that the preliminary analyses had shown to be correlated with the decision to release on parole licence were entered. The statistical model selected seven of these variables:[86]

- actuarial ROR of a serious offence during the parole period (three categories: 0%–7%, 8%–16%, 17% and higher)

- prisoner security category (B, C, D, Closed YOI, female)

- SPO states that offending behaviour courses have been completed (Yes, No, Not mentioned)

- SPO recommendation (YES, NO, No clear recommendation)

- HPO recommendation (YES, NO, No clear recommendation)

- number of adjudications in prison (none, 1–3, 4 or more)

- previous convictions of a sexual or violent nature (none, a sex or violence conviction, or both).

As Table 6.1 illustrates, the statistical model correctly predicted the decisions made by the Board in 85.1 per cent of cases: 84.1 per cent of YES decisions and 85.5 per cent of NO decisions.

---

86   For full details of the model, see Appendix 1. The statistical model selected the variables using the stepwise procedure based on the likelihood ratio statistic. The cut-off level for YES/NO prediction was set at 0.4. Three other variables considered which were not selected by the model were: type of offence; breach of probation/CSO etc.; and breach of bail.

Table 6.1:   Actual parole decisions compared with predicted parole decisions

Actual panel decision*	Predicted panel decision		Percentage of decisions correctly predicted
	YES	NO	
YES (145)	122	23	84.1
NO (283)	41	242	85.5
Number predicted	163	265	
Percentage of predictions released/not released	74.9	91.3	85.1

* Ten cases excluded due to missing data.

Probability scores for each case, derived from the combination of weights assigned to these seven variables, were grouped into five probability bands ranging from zero to 20 per cent to greater than 80 per cent to 100 per cent.

Table 6.2:   Parole decisions related to statistical probability of refusal (five levels)

Probability of release on parole	Number of cases	Number and percentage granted parole		Percentage of cases in each probability band
		Number	Percentage	
20% or below	208	9	4.3	48.6
>20%–40%	57	14	24.6	13.3
>40%–60%	45	25	55.6	10.5
>60%–80%	46	33	71.7	10.7
>80%	72	64	88.9	16.8
Total	428*	145	33.9	100

* Ten cases excluded due to missing data.

It can be seen from Table 6.2 that:

● Nearly half the prisoners (48.6%) had a very low probability of release (between zero and 20%), and in fact only 4.3 per cent were released. In other words, half the cases considered by the Board stood almost no chance of being paroled.

● At the other end of the scale, one in six (16.8%) had a very high probability of parole (more than 80%), of whom 88.9 per cent were paroled.

- Taking these together, the parole decisions were correctly predicted for 65.4 per cent of prisoners 94 per cent of the time.[87]

- 'Fifty-fifty' cases (probability of parole greater than 40% up to 60%) were a small minority (10.5%) of cases considered by the Board. Of these around half (55.6%) were paroled.

In Table 6.3 the top and bottom probability bands are further subdivided. It shows that in about one in ten cases parole was almost guaranteed (95% were paroled). At the other end of the scale, nearly one in three cases (29.7%) had a probability of release of 2.5 per cent or less. Only one of them was in fact released. Thus, the parole decision for four out of ten of the prisoners considered by the Parole Board was predicted with almost total accuracy from seven characteristics of the cases that were easily identified from the dossier.

Table 6.3: Parole decision by probability of refusal (high and low bands)

Probability of release on parole	Number of cases	Number and percentage granted parole		Percentage of cases in each probability band
		Number	Percentage	
2.5% or below	127	1	0.8	29.7
>2.5%–5%	27	2	7.4	6.3
>5%–10%	27	2	7.4	6.3
>10%–20%	27	4	14.8	6.3
>80%–90%	34	24	82.4	7.9
>90%–100%	38	44	94.7	8.9

This model turned out to be a very powerful predictor of Parole Board decision-making.[88] There is no doubt that an even more powerful model could be constructed if data relating to willingness and progress in addressing offending behaviour and its relationship to risk reduction were to be more clearly presented in the dossiers. For this would certainly be a better predictor than the information on whether courses had been completed or not which was extracted for the present exercise from seconded probation officers' reports.

As an example of what might be achieved if this information were provided more systematically in the dossier, the researchers coded from the panel's reasons whether or not the prisoner was said to have been willing to address various aspects of his/her offending

---

87   This can easily be calculated from Table 6.2. Of those with a probability of release of greater than 80 percent (16.8% of the total) eight were not released. Of those with a probability of release of 20 per cent or less (48.6% of the sample), nine were released. So only 17 of these 280 decisions (6.1%) were wrongly predicted.

88   When the PBIM's report on whether courses had been completed or not was added to the original model, the discriminant power hardly changed. It decreased slightly to 84.9 per cent, but the model was slightly worse at predicting YES decisions (81.1%) and slightly better (86.1%) at predicting NO decisions.

behaviour and to have made progress in doing so.[89] When this information was added to the logistic regression, the discriminant power of the model increased to 91.1 per cent (88.3% of YES decisions correctly predicted and 92.6% of NO decisions). As a result, it was possible to predict correctly 97 per cent of the parole decisions made for 85 per cent of the prisoners in the sample.

Predicting decisions relating to sex offenders

Multiple logistic regression analysis was also used to develop a model specifically to predict release decisions for sex offenders, who are of particular concern to the Board. The same variables were entered as for the general model, plus completion of SOTP and denial of the offence. The best model selected only the home probation officer's recommendation.[90] As Table 6.4 shows, this model correctly predicted 87 per cent of parole decisions: 94.4 per cent of YES decisions and 85.1 per cent of NO decisions.

Table 6.4: Actual parole decisions for sex offenders compared with predicted decisions

Actual panel decision	Predicted panel decision		Percentage of decisions correctly predicted
	YES	NO	
YES (18)	17	1	94.4
NO (74)	11	63	85.1
Number predicted	28	64	
Percentage of predictions released/not released	60.7	98.4	87.0

Only one of the 18 YES decisions made by the Parole Board concerned a sex offender who was predicted not to be released – he had not been recommended by his home probation officer. On the other hand, 11 of the 28 sex offenders (39%) predicted to be released (that is they had a positive HPO report) were nevertheless kept in custody. This again illustrates the difference between probation officers' views on the benefits of parole and the Parole Board's interpretation of the directions it has been given relating to the avoidance of risk.

---

89 Six variables were added from statements made in the reasons given by panels. They were: willingness to address offending behaviour; sufficient progress made with offending behaviour; willingness to address drugs or alcohol; sufficient progress made in addressing drugs or alcohol; willingness to do SOTP; sufficient progress in SOTP. Two of these variables were selected by the model: sufficient progress made with offending behaviour; and sufficient progress made in addressing drugs or alcohol.

90 See above page 44. See also Appendix 1.

Using the model to explain ethnic disparities in parole rates

The statistical model outlined above predicts parole decisions on the basis of variables, all of which it is proper for the Parole Board to take into account. It is possible to use such a model as a 'matching device' in order to explore whether apparent differences in parole rates for various groups of prisoners can be explained by legally relevant factors. A major objective of the Parole Board is to ensure that cases are dealt with in a consistent and equitable manner. It is particularly concerned that its decisions should be patently non-discriminatory. It was therefore important to try to explain why, in this sample of parole decisions, the parole rate varied considerably between ethnic groups: 73 per cent of Asian prisoners were paroled, 32 per cent of whites and 28 per cent of black prisoners.[91]

The first point to make is that listening to discussions on more than 400 prisoners only one remark was heard which referred to the race, ethnicity, colour or cultural background of the prisoner under consideration and this remark was not intended to disadvantage the prisoner concerned. To what extent, then, could the very much higher paroling rate for Asians than for white and black prisoners be explained by characteristics relevant to parole decisions for all prisoners, irrespective of their ethnic origin? One must, of course, bear in mind the small number of Asians (22) in the sample. Nevertheless, it was found that the Asian prisoners were more likely (because they had on average less serious criminal histories) to be in the lowest ROR risk band (0–7%); to have no adjudications in prison; and to have finished any courses mentioned in the seconded probation officer's report. As a consequence, they were more likely to be recommended for parole by both seconded and home probation officers.

This is reflected in the much higher proportion of Asian prisoners falling into the category with a high probability of being paroled.

- Sixty-eight per cent of Asian prisoners had variables associated with a probability of release on parole of more than 60 per cent, compared with 26 per cent of white prisoners and 19 per cent of black prisoners.

- Only 27 per cent of Asians had variables associated with a probability of release on parole of 40 per cent or less, compared with 63 per cent of whites and 69 per cent of blacks.

- Taking parole relevant variables into account, the 'expected' parole rate for Asian prisoners was 65.5 per cent compared with the 'observed' parole rate of 73 per cent.[92] This is not a statistically significant difference, given the small number of cases.

- Thus, the different parole rates appear to be well explained by the extent to which the different ethnic groups met the criteria used by the Board.

91 Asian includes Pakistani, Indian and Bangladeshi. Black includes Caribbean and African.
92 The expected rate for Afro-Caribbean prisoners was 27 per cent, the same as the observed rate. For whites the expected rate was 33 per cent and the observed rate 32 per cent.

However, it was not possible on the basis of this research to know whether the differential parole rates would be found in a much larger sample of parole decisions. Nor was it possible to determine the reasons why the Asian prisoners in the sample fared so much better in relation to offending-behaviour courses in prison. The Prison Service is aware of the need for ethnic monitoring to ensure equal access to resources for prisoners and it is obviously important that no ethnic group should have less opportunity to be able to meet the criteria demanded by the parole system. We recommend that a sophisticated statistical model of the kind devised for this study be used to monitor parole decisions in relation to ethnicity, gender and other variables which should have no relevance to the parole decision.

Conclusion

The predictability of parole decisions revealed by this chapter, combined with the evidence presented in Chapter 3 on the concordance between members' decisions and the time taken to reach them, inevitably raise questions about the current way in which the Parole Board conducts its business. The implications of these findings for policy will be explored in Chapter 8.

Chapter 7   The role, use and value of PBIM reports

The purpose of the PBIM interview

Under the old parole system prisoners were interviewed by a member of the Local Review Committee, whose task was to help the prisoner put his or her case for parole. In 1988 the Carlisle Committee, which recommended the abolition of LRCs, suggested that this interviewing role should be taken up by 'a group of local people who might be termed *parole counsellors*' whose task would be 'to study the [prisoner's] dossier, talk over the main points with them and help them in putting down in writing their own comments'.[93] This suggestion was not adopted and instead some Parole Board members[94] have been designated as Parole Board Interviewing Members (PBIMs).

The PBIM's task is more complex than that of the former LRC members and certainly different from the 'counselling' role envisaged by Carlisle. According to the Guidance Note issued to PBIMs by the Parole Board, the purpose of the interview is as follows:

- To ensure that the prisoner understands the parole procedures.

- To check on the accuracy, contents and quality of the dossier, to ensure that the prisoner has read and understood it, and to enable him or her to challenge any matter contained in it.

- To obtain on behalf of members of the panel, clarification or expansion of any matters which will assist them in assessment of risk, reaching their decision and framing licence conditions.

- To enable the prisoner to clarify or expand upon any matters which he or she wishes to be drawn to the attention of the panel, and otherwise add verbally to any written representations.

In addition, there are specific instructions on the arrangements for the interview; the explanation to the prisoner of the role of the PBIM interview and report; the structure and coverage of the interview; and the formulation of the PBIM report to the Board.

---

93   Carlisle (1988), paras 338-341.
94   The independent, probation and criminologist members, but not judicial or psychiatrist members.

Our observations of 151 interviews confirmed that, within the time allocated (usually about an hour), PBIMs did their best to follow the pattern laid down in the Guidance Note. They emphasised that the report was meant to be 'factual' or 'objective' and that they would not be expressing opinions or making recommendations. Several told the prisoner:

It's a chance to give your side.

The interview is your opportunity to have your say.

When you're speaking to me you're speaking to the Board.

When asked to rank, in order of importance, the purposes of the interview listed above, 16 of the 53 PBIMs said that they were all of equal importance. Taking this into account[95] it was found that:

● *clarifying matters for the Board which will assist it in assessment of risk* was ranked first by 87 per cent of the PBIMs

● *checking the accuracy of the dossier* was ranked first by 47 per cent of PBIMs

● *helping the prisoner to make representations* was ranked first by 36 per cent

● *ensuring the prisoner understands parole procedures* was ranked first by only 30 per cent.

The relatively low ranking given to helping the prisoner to make representations and to understand parole procedures needs to be evaluated in the light of the fact that many fewer prisoners than formerly make their own written representations. Of the prisoners interviewed in this study, only a third said they had done so. It is likely that many assumed that the PBIM interview was the best way to make representations.

Views on the interview

Both PBIMs and prisoners had positive things to say about the interview. PBIMs felt that more than 80 per cent of the interviews had helped the prisoner to present his/her case and that nearly all the prisoners had been co-operative and respectful. For their part, a high proportion of prisoners (more than 80%) said that the PBIM had been respectful, fair-minded, willing to listen and had asked the right questions: they would not have preferred this task to be carried out by any other person.

Amongst the sample of prisoners who had recently been refused parole, the proportion expressing such laudatory views was a good deal lower. Nonetheless, at least half still had positive things to say, although 40 per cent said they would have preferred someone else to

95   Where purposes were ranked equal first, each one was counted separately as a first choice.

have conducted the interview. Yet none of the tracked and only five of the refused men (even when prompted) were in favour of this interview being assigned to a seconded probation officer.

There were, however, some complaints. About a third of the tracked prisoners said that the interview had been 'rushed': indeed, PBIMs thought that 40 per cent of prisoners would have regarded them as 'rushed'. Usually the interview took around an hour but for some prisoners this was not thought long enough. Two-thirds of those who said that they had felt rushed had in fact been given between 55 and 65 minutes. It seemed to our observers that, allowing for delays in bringing prisoners to the interview, no more than two could be completed, without a feeling of being rushed, within a three-hour period. This means that it would be unwise for PBIMs to schedule more than four interviews in one day.

According to both prisoners and PBIMs, four out of ten inmates had been nervous or upset during the interview. Indeed, about a third of prisoners said that they had not managed to get over all the points they wanted to make. These tensions were revealed in the transcripts of the interviews. Despite attempts by PBIMs to ask 'open-ended' questions in the hope of eliciting a full response, all too often they received a short single-sentence answer from a prisoner who found the occasion too stressful to be able to make the best of his/her case for parole.

Evaluations of the interview

PBIMs said that 90 per cent of the interviews they had conducted with the tracked prisoners had yielded relevant new information, not available in the dossier, which would assist the parole panel in its assessment of risk. They also said that 80 per cent of the interviews had enabled them to make a better assessment than was possible from the dossier alone of the prisoner's motivation to change and insight into his/her offending behaviour.

The information gathered in half of the interviews was considered by the PBIM to be sufficiently significant to affect the prisoner's chance of parole: in 32 per cent of cases to have decreased it and in 22 per cent to have increased it. But when asked how much difference it might make, very few said it would make 'a lot' of difference.

The prisoners were more optimistic about the impact that the interview might have on the Parole Board. Forty-five per cent thought that it had increased their chance of parole and only six per cent (compared with 22% of PBIMs) thought it had decreased their chance.

The PBIMs were able to make a good assessment of the prisoners' prospects of parole – perhaps not surprisingly given the predictability of parole decisions and their experience as panel members. Seventy-nine per cent of those whose chance they rated 'high' or 'very high' were paroled compared with eight per cent of those whose chance they rated 'moderate' or 'low'.

What difference did the PBIM report make to decisions at the Board?

It is clear that PBIMs and prisoners believed that the interviews 'made a difference' in a sufficient number of cases for them to have been worthwhile. To what extent were they correct? The fact that it had been possible to construct, without recourse to material in the PBIM report, a model of decision-making that predicted 85 per cent of parole decisions, obviously raises a grave doubt.

PBIM reports were rarely referred to during the observed panel discussions: indeed in only ten per cent of the 417 cases observed. But panel members were asked about the PBIM report in the questionnaire attached to each dossier. Critical remarks were made about only six per cent of the reports, whereas 15 per cent received words of praise. The researchers sought to ascertain from panel members whether the PBIM report had:

- *changed* the pre-panel decision that they would have made if the PBIM report had not been available in the dossier

- *confirmed* the pre-panel decision

- *added nothing* which influenced the pre-panel decision reached on the basis of other information in the dossier.

The responses of lead members were analysed in relation to the 346 cases where they had completed the form. This revealed that:

- In only 29 assessments (8.4%) did the lead member say that his or her mind had been changed by something in the PBIM report.

- In 76 per cent the lead member said the PBIM report confirmed a decision already reached on the basis of other evidence in the dossier.

- In 16 per cent the PBIM report was said to have had no influence at all on the pre-panel decision, because the decision was already so 'clear-cut that the PBIM could add nothing'.[96]

Lead members' assessments of the impact of the report on their decisions were analysed in relation to 100 cases where the PBIM had told the researchers that useful new information had emerged. In only a minority of these cases – 11 per cent – did the lead member say that his or her pre-panel decision had been changed by the PBIM report. Indeed, 14 per cent said it had added nothing, while the remaining three-quarters said that it confirmed what they had decided on the basis of other information in the dossier.

---

96   The results were exactly the same when the 1,038 responses made by all panel members (relating to 410 cases) were analysed. It is worth noting that the 'PBIM report added nothing' judgements were not evenly distributed among the 45 panel members who completed the questionnaires. Four panel members accounted for more than half of these judgements.

This data confirms the conclusion that PBIM reports had, at most, a marginal impact on parole decision-making.

In what ways and in which direction did PBIM reports influence decisions?

An analysis was made of the 29 cases where the lead member said that the PBIM report had changed the decision that would have been made on the basis of the other information in the dossier. The PBIM report more often changed the pre-panel decision from YES to NO (18 cases)[97] than from NO to YES (11 cases). Bearing in mind that this finding is based on only a small number of cases, it would be worth investigating whether, in a larger sample of cases, PBIM reports are more likely to be interpreted in a way which is unfavourable rather than favourable to a prisoner's chances of parole.

Yet, whatever conclusions one might reach on the basis of a statistical analysis of parole decision-making, it is clear that a large majority of panel members took the view that the PBIM report was useful to them. Occasionally it changed their mind, but far more often it helped them to feel more confident that they had come to the right conclusion. Only one member, in response to the questionnaire, consistently maintained that the PBIM report 'added nothing'. He wrote: 'too subjective as it is based on the interview'.

Board members, in answering the questionnaire, identified two ways in which they believed the PBIM report had assisted them. First, it sometimes brought to light new factual information, such as a recent MDT failure, continuing drug use or unrecorded previous convictions. Indeed, such information was observed being voluntarily given to the PBIM by the prisoners:

Case 44: [SPO/HPO NO, RORS 10 per cent, RORA 29 per cent, serving eight years for aggravated burglary, first review. Panel decided NO]

PBIM: *Have you used drugs recently?* Inmate: *Yes, last night.* PBIM: *Are you bombed out now?* Inmate: *No.* PBIM: *What did you have? Are you affected by this?* Inmate: *No – nobody is.* PBIM: *You think that using drugs is OK?* Inmate: *No opinion.*

Two panel members wrote that the PBIM report had **confirmed** the NO decision they were inclined to reach on the basis of other information in the dossier decision. One wrote *that the revelation that the inmate took cannabis the night before was the final clincher.* The third panel member wrote that the PBIM report had **added nothing** to her conclusion, based on other material in the dossier, that the prisoner was too high a risk to release on parole.

---

97   Where they had been initially inclined to a YES but on reading the PBIM's report changed their mind to NO, that NO decision was confirmed by the other two panel members in every case. And in none of those cases had the other two panel members said that the PBIM report had changed their mind.

Case 123: [SPO/HPO YES, RORS 8 per cent, RORA 19 per cent, serving eight years for robbery, second review. Panel decided NO]

PBIM: *On the 1st January this year, you refused to give a sample at a MDT.* Inmate: *I told them I'm straight. I didn't want to waste their money. I don't do Class A drugs.* PBIM: *So do you take cannabis on a regular basis?* Inmate: *No.* PBIM: *When did you last take it?* Inmate: *Two weeks ago.*

Two panel members noted that the PBIM report had **changed** their decision from YES to NO. One said: *Until I learned he was still using cannabis I was inclined to agree parole, but his admission to the PBIM that he had used cannabis two weeks before, suggested he was still not prepared to obey the rules.* The other wrote: *This information on cannabis use and the explanation of knife in cell changed my decision from YES to 'maybe wish to discuss the relevance of this to risk with my colleagues'.* The third member indicated that the PBIM report had **confirmed** her NO decision.

Only two PBIMs were observed to caution the inmate before questioning him:

This is a standard warning I give to everyone. Think before you speak. It will all go in the report, so don't say it if you don't want it to go in the report.

Secondly, PBIM reports were said to have been useful because of the insight they had given the panel member into the prisoners' attitudes and risk potential. The flavour of their remarks showed that the prisoner was judged, more often than not, to his/her disadvantage:

Case 125: [SPO/HPO YES, RORS 15 per cent, RORA 31 per cent, serving six years for robbery. Panel decided NO]

Two panel members indicated that the PBIM report had **changed** their decision from YES to NO. One gave no reason, the other wrote: *SPO report was very positive, well presented, but the answers given by the inmate to the PBIM show a level of immaturity not shown in the SPO report. Since the PBIM reported verbatim for several questions, these have altered my opinion as to whether he can 'hack it' for such a long licence.* The third member noted that the report had **confirmed** his NO decision: *Reassuring.*

Case 142: [SPO NO, HPO NO REC., RORS 18 per cent, RORA 33 per cent, serving four years six months for robbery. Panel decided NO]

All three panel members wrote that the PBIM **confirmed** their NO decisions, making the following comments:

Useful exploration of important issues helped convey the level of immaturity.

It was revealing as to his attitudes and also showed up a poor relationship with his HPO.

It gave a more direct impression of the inmate and his attitude/view.

Case 238: [SPO/HPO YES, RORS 6 per cent, RORA 17 per cent, serving five years six months for burglary. Panel decided YES]

One panel member noted the PBIM report had **changed** her decision from NO to YES: *The PBIM report clarified issues and gave a good overview of the prisoner's view. I was inclined to reject but changed my view after reading the PBIM report.* A second member wrote that it had **confirmed** his decision which prior to the panel had been NO: *It confirms that there are still unanswered questions – and that he remains an unpredictable man – where I would assess the ROR to be fairly high.* The third member indicated that the report had **added nothing**: *I didn't feel there was any new material offered, though it did offer clarity.*

Case 458: [SPO/HPO YES, RORS 3 per cent, RORA 6 per cent, serving seven years for death by reckless driving, second review. Panel decided NO]

Two panel members **changed** from YES to NO. One wrote: *A very difficult case with wildly different reports and assessments. The PPA [Prison Officer's Report] and PBIM were negative indicating a poor attitude. Probation reports were very positive. I was just swung to NO by his attitude.* The other noted: *A clarification of last adjudication – seven days in the 'seg' and the admission 'I refused work' were important. Also reference to removal from drug-free wing.* The third member wrote: *PBIM report contributed to my decision.*

In other words, panel members sometimes made subjective judgements about prisoners on the basis of a reported interview, with no possibility of asking the PBIM or the prisoner whether their interpretation was correct. This is an inevitable consequence of a system that does not allow a personal hearing with representation before the final decision-making body.

Implications

These findings about the role of the PBIM will, no doubt, be uncomfortable for many Board members, but they reflect the reality of parole as it operates under the present strict risk-aversive approach. They raise the question of whether the considerable cost in fees and travelling expenses of sending Parole Board Interviewing Members to prisons to conduct these interviews can be justified. If not, what system should be put in its place to ensure that prisoners are provided with the assistance they need to make an application for parole? And who should be responsible for reviewing the quality of the dossier to ensure that Parole Board decisions are based on as full, up-to-date and valid information as possible?

Chapter 8   Conclusions and implications for policy

The use made of parole

The restructuring of the parole system, introduced by the Criminal Justice Act 1991, was largely based on recommendations from the Carlisle Committee which were intended to bring greater rationality to the system, fairer procedures and decisions based on the criterion of risk. The Committee had expected that these changes would be accompanied by a greater willingness of the Parole Board to grant parole. The assumption was that, by moving the eligibility threshold for parole from a third to half the sentence, the demands of deterrence and retribution would, by that stage, have been met for most prisoners. Only a relatively small proportion of high-risk prisoners would be denied parole in order to protect the public. For them the period of licence introduced after two-thirds of the sentence would act as a 'failsafe' to ensure that they would not be 'released cold' into community. But it was not intended to operate as a 'substitute' for parole for other prisoners. It was to be a way of prolonging the supervisory element of their parole licence so as to better protect the public. The Committee put it this way:

> In proposing enhanced supervision requirements [after two-thirds of the sentence] and the restoration of meaning to the full sentence we believe that it will be possible to provide greater protection for the public, while also enabling a higher proportion of long-term offenders to be judged suitable for release from prison at the half-way point of their sentence.[98]

This expectation has not been met. The proportion of prisoners granted parole at some point of their sentence has fallen from around 70 per cent under the old system to less than a half now.[99] Why has this happened? There is no doubt that the emphasis placed on risk in successive versions of the Secretary of State's directions (and consequently in training for Parole Board members) has created a generally cautious approach. But it is also true, as this research has shown, that Parole Board members often believe that the risk of reconviction during the parole licence period is substantially higher than that indicated by the actuarially-based risk of reconviction score (ROR) which is based on a reliable follow-up study. Furthermore, Parole Board members appear to take the view that the extended period of supervision implicit in release on parole cannot in many cases provide any significant reassurance that the risk of reoffending will be reduced. They also often preferred prisoners to complete offending behaviour courses in prison, rather than under parole supervision in the community. In fact, it was found that half the prisoners in the sample of decisions observed had a risk of being reconvicted for a serious offence while on parole licence of

---

98 Carlisle (1988), para. 280.
99 It will be recalled that if the Carlisle Committee's recommendation had been followed, those sentenced to four years' imprisonment would not have been included in the DCR system and so would have been automatically released after serving half the sentence.

seven per cent or less – equivalent to an average of four prisoners in every 100 being reconvicted of an offence that would be likely to lead to imprisonment. Yet the Board paroled only half of these low-risk prisoners. This approach inevitably has cost implications: prisoners are refused parole who might, on a more realistic interpretation of risk, be released. For example, if the Board were to release those prisoners who are not only low risk but are recommended by both their prison-based and their home probation officer, the parole rate would increase by more than a quarter – but without any increase in the average reconviction rate of parolees as a whole. The effect over a year would be to release approximately 550 more prisoners on parole, 96 per cent of whom would not be predicted to commit a serious offence while on parole licence. Policy makers may wish to consider whether the savings which would probably be produced by a higher parole rate could be used to provide additional support for work in prisons and the community which would help prisoners address more adequately their offending behaviour.

In a system which gives priority to risk, it is essential that risk should be assessed as accurately as possible, both to protect the public and to ensure that the liberty of prisoners who do not pose a high risk to the public is not unnecessarily restricted. After all, the period normally available for parole is equivalent to at least a 16-month sentence of imprisonment. There appears therefore to be a strong case for again making available to Parole Board members the actuarial risk of reconviction score (suitably updated) for each prisoner. Bearing in mind that, when it was available, little use appears to have been made of it, Board members could be directed specifically to give weight to the actuarial ROR in light of the recommendations of professionals who have a first-hand knowledge of the prisoner.

In terms of parole procedures, the DCR system is regarded by prisoners as fairer and more open than the old parole system, although prisoners still know too little about the criteria they have to meet in order to be granted parole. The steps being taken to try to remedy this are to be welcomed. Yet it has to be recognised that the majority of prisoners who were refused parole thought that the reasons they were given were unfair. Very few regarded them as a spur to a more positive approach to their remaining period in prison and many resented the fact that although they had been denied parole they still faced stringent licence conditions when they came to be released after serving two-thirds of their sentence. These reactions to the system may, in part, be a result of the low parole rate for, as this research has shown, a substantial minority of those refused parole had had their hopes built up by positive recommendations from both the seconded and the home probation officer – only to have them dashed by the Board. There is clearly a danger that too great a restriction of parole may foster negative attitudes and undermine efforts made in prison to encourage prisoners to change their patterns of criminal behaviour. This is another reason for reconsidering the rate at which parole is granted.

Streamlining decision-making?

At the Board

As this study has shown, the Secretary of State's directions and the way in which Parole Board members interpreted them, resulted in a highly predictable pattern of decisions. When Parole Board panels met, the three members expressed no differences of view about the decision in four out of five cases. Moreover, in only seven cases in every 100 was the decision different from that initially suggested by the member who introduced the case. A statistical analysis showed that two-thirds of the prisoners had characteristics – easily extracted from their dossier – which predicted, with 94 per cent accuracy, whether or not they would be paroled.

This high degree of concordance, and the rarity with which dissenting opinions were expressed at panel meetings, naturally raises the question of whether it is necessary for all cases to be referred to panels meeting in London, with all the expense that that entails. Some consideration might therefore be given to whether it is possible to 'streamline' the decision-making process. Where all three members agree that the prisoner should be paroled there appears to be no good reason for them to travel to London for a meeting. The reasons and licence conditions could be agreed through electronic communication and no due process issues would be likely to arise. The minority of cases (about 10%) where panel members were not in agreement would, of course, need to be discussed at a meeting.

But what about cases where all three members say NO to parole? Here, use could be made of a 'decision predictor', of the kind developed for this study (but not, of course, necessarily based on the same paroling rate), to identify those cases which ought to be discussed at a meeting. It would need to be validated on a larger sample of cases and improved, if possible, through better quality information on the satisfactory completion of offending behaviour courses. Where all three members are agreed that parole should not be granted and the decision predictor confirms that in the past the chance of such a prisoner being released was negligible, a meeting would not be likely to lead to a different decision. However, for the relatively small number of cases where the predictor indicates that such a prisoner might be paroled (probably between 5% and 10% of cases[100]), it would not be appropriate to accept negative decisions on parole without the cases being reconsidered by a *different* three-member panel. This would provide a kind of 'internal appeal' in which the members of the new panel would be aware that they would need to weigh particularly carefully the arguments for and against parole. The overall effect might be to increase the rate of parole among these cases. Again, it would only be necessary to convene a meeting of this second panel where there is disagreement.

On the basis of the observations made in this study, it is estimated that the total number of cases that would need to be discussed at panel meetings would be around ten to 15 per cent of the current caseload.

---

100   See Table 6.2 on page 64 above. Of the 118 prisoners with a predicted probability of release greater than 60 per cent, only 21 (17.8%) were refused parole. Of the 163 with a probability of release of greater than 40 per cent, 41 (25%) were refused parole – only about 10 per cent of the caseload in our sample of observed cases (42 of 428). This is the group we have in mind to be reconsidered by a new panel if parole were refused.

Interviewing prisoners

The findings of this research raise questions about the value of the Parole Board Members' interviews with prisoners and the reports they submit to the Board. However well PBIMs carried out their task, there was little scope for what they wrote or discovered to affect the parole decision in the majority of cases. Indeed, in relation to only one in 12 cases did a Board member say that his or her mind had been changed as a result of something in the PBIM's report.

If it were to be concluded that employing Board Members to interview prisoners and write reports is an expense that cannot be justified, some of the PBIM's tasks would have to be carried out by others. The job of ensuring that dossiers are complete, and that all the material that the prisoner regards as relevant to his/her application is included, could be made the responsibility of parole clerks, although they would need to be supported more effectively than at present by the prison administration. But someone else would need to ensure that the prisoner is familiar with parole procedures and with the criteria that the Board has been directed to apply, that the prisoner has read and understood the dossier and is in a position to challenge any matter contained in it, and that he or she has had all the help needed to make effective representations to the Board. Policy makers might consider whether these tasks could be passed to voluntary, independent and trained parole counsellors, recruited by each prison from retired probation officers and others with relevant experience. This would have the advantage that the parole counsellor could first meet the prisoner early in the sentence to explain the system and to work out how best the prisoner might try to meet the parole criteria. Subsequently, the counsellor could meet the prisoner to review his or her progress as reflected in the dossier and assist with representations. Whatever solution may be considered, it is vital that the procedural protections available to prisoners are not diminished.

Some broader implications for policy

The parole system is, in essence, a means whereby a sentence of imprisonment imposed by a court can be operated with a degree of flexibility as regards the proportion of the sentence to be served in custody rather than under conditions of licence in the community. As such, it cannot be considered in isolation from the general structure and level of prison sentences. The Carlisle Committee had no mandate to review sentencing policy as such. But it recognised that its proposals to bring 'truth to sentencing', by making all parts of the sentence 'count', had the potential to increase the 'quantum of punishment' that a prison sentence would entail. In its opinion, sentence lengths would therefore need to be reduced so as to reflect the real burden of a sentence of imprisonment. This was recognised in 1992 by the Lord Chief Justice when he issued a Practice Direction reminding the courts to take into account that the meaning of a long-term prison sentence had changed.[101]

---

101 *Practice Statement (Crime: Sentencing)* [1992] 1 WLR 948.

However, there has been a modest increase in the average length of sentences imposed in the Crown Court and a substantial increase in the number of long-term prisoners in custody.[102] At the same time, the 'quantum of punishment' has risen further through the attachment of a greater number of licence conditions both to those paroled and, on their eventual release from custody, to those denied parole. It is in this light that the dramatic decline in the use of parole in recent years should be evaluated.

---

102   See *Prison Statistics for England and Wales* 1998 (1999), Cm 4430, paras 1.16 and 4.12.

Appendix 1

Models of multivariate logistic regression predicting parole decisions

The model for the full sample.

428 cases (10 rejected because of missing data). YES/NO decisions based on a cut-off of 0.4. Discriminant power 85.05 per cent (84.14% of YES decisions, 85.51% of NO decisions).

Variable	ß	S.E.	Significance	Odds ratio
ROR[1]			.0000	
ROR 8%–16%	-1.0655	.3570	.0028	.6937
ROR 17% and higher	-2.2689	.5521	.0000	.3052
Prison category[2]			.0170	
C	.9631	.7439	.1954	2.6198
D	1.7248	.7967	.0253	5.9432
Closed YOI	2.4667	.9626	.0104	11.7836
Female	.5546	1.1656	.7447	1.7413
Offending behaviour courses[3]			.0077	
Not finished	-.9458	.3230	.0034	.3884
Not mentioned	.3433	.7576	.6505	1.4095
SPO recommendation[4]			.0147	
No	-1.7993	.6782	.0080	.1654
No recommendation/ no report	-.8242	.5812	.1562	.4386
HPO recommendation[5]			.0004	
No	-3.1419	1.1248	.0052	.0432
No recommendation/ no report	-2.1430	.7378	.0037	.1173
Adjudications[6]			.0000	
1 to 3	-.7542	.3801	.0472	.4704
4 or more	-1.9551	.4235	.0000	.1415
Previous convictions: sex/violence[7]			.0252	
Either	-.6200	.3196	.0524	.5379
Both	1.1952	.8266	.1482	3.3042
Constant	-2.3.88	.5785	.0001	

1 Reference category is those whose ROR was 0%–7%.
2 Reference category is those whose prison category was B.
3 Reference category is those where the SPO said in his/her report that the inmate had finished the courses mentioned in his/her report.
4 Reference category is those where the SPO recommended the prisoner for parole.
5 Reference category is those where the HPO recommended the prisoner for parole.
6 Reference category is those who had no prison adjudications on current sentence.
7 Reference category is those who had no previous sexual or violent convictions.

Model for sex offenders only.

92 cases. YES/NO decisions based on a cut-off of 0.4. Discriminant power 86.96 per cent (94.44% of YES decisions, 85.14% of NO decisions).

Variable	ß	S.E.	Significance	Odds ratio
HPO recommendation[1]			.0002	
No	-4.4427	1.0807	.0000	.0118
No recommendation/ no report	-9.6381	35.2268	.7844	.0001
Constant	-4.2583	11.7471	.7170	

1   Reference category is those where the HPO recommended the prisoner for parole.

Appendix 2

The relationship between selected variables and the parole rate

Variable	Category (and number in category)	Percentage paroled	Significance
Race	White (340)	31.8	.000
	Black (69)	27.5	
	Asian (22)	72.7	
	Other (7)	57.1	
Sex of inmate	Male (431)	32.9	.032
	Female (7)	71.4	
Number of adjudications	None (134)	53.7	.000
	1–3 (151)	35.1	
	4 or more (153)	14.4	
Actuarial ROR (serious offences on parole licence)	0–2% (83)	57.8	.000
	3%–4% (67)	46.3	
	5%–7% (76)	46.1	
	8%–10% (62)	21.0	
	11%–16% (62)	21.0	
	17% and higher (87)	8.0	
Number of previous convictions	None (65)	61.5	.000
	1–5 (146)	45.9	
	6–10 (71)	26.8	
	11 or more (155)	13.5	
Number of previous probation/CSO or other supervisory sentence	None (184)	51.6	.000
	One (72)	29.2	
	Two or more (181)	17.1	
Number of previous youth custody	None (245)	45.3	.000
	One or more (82)	25.6	
Number of previous adult custody	None (259)	44.4	.000
	One to four (133)	22.6	
	Five or more (45)	4.4	

Variable	Category (and number in category)	Percentage paroled	Significance
Previous violent or sexual convictions	Neither (198)	48.0	.000
	Either violent or sexual (225)	21.3	
	Both (14)	28.6	
Previous breach of probation/CSO etc	Yes (133)	18.8	.000
	No (120)	22.5	
	DNA no previous order (184)	51.6	
Previous breach of bail	Yes (132)	20.5	.000
	No/DNA (306)	39.2	
Breach of home leave/ temporary release on current sentence	Yes (13)	15.4	.159
	No (425)	34.1	
Previous parole supervision failure	Yes (14)	14.3	.121
	No (424)	34.2	
Age at first conviction	14 or under (118)	22.0	.000
	15 to 16 (82)	22.0	
	17 to 19 (103)	41.7	
	20 to 29 (73)	39.7	
	30 and over (62)	50.0	
Age at current conviction	21 or under (73)	38.4	.738
	22 to 29 (168)	31.5	
	30 to 39 (121)	34.7	
	40 and over (76)	31.6	
SPO recommendation	Yes (267)	50.6	.000
	No (121)	3.3	
	No recommendation/no report (50)	16.0	
HPO recommendation	Yes (286)	49.7	.000
	No (110)	1.8	
	No recommendation/no report (42)	7.1	
SPO report and courses	Courses mentioned in report are completed (160)	55.0	.000
	Courses are not completed / not mentioned (270)	21.1	
SPO report and willingness to address offending behaviour	SPO says inmate is willing (368)	38.0	.000
	SPO says inmate unwilling (57)	5.3	
	SPO does not mention willingness (5)	40.0	

Variable	Category (and number in category)	Percentage paroled	Significance
Denial of offence	Inmate does not deny offence (384)	35.9	.005
	Inmate does deny offence (54)	16.7	
Marital status on release	Married/cohabiting (111)	33.3	.953
	Single (327)	33.6	
Offence type	Import drugs (22)	77.3	.000
	Other drug offence(54)	50.0	
	Personal violence (92)	33.7	
	Robbery (96)	30.2	
	Sex offences against minors (41)	19.5	
	Sex offences against adults (51)	19.6	
	Arson (6)	66.7	
	Burglary (53)	20.8	
	Theft/handling (12)	33.3	
	Fraud/deception (7)	42.9	
	Other (4)	75.0	
Sentence length	4 years (107)	37.4	.727
	>4 years to 5 years (128)	32.0	
	>5 years to 6 years (57)	36.8	
	>6 years to 9 years (115)	32.2	
	Over 9 years (31)	25.8	
Employment available on release	Yes (124)	47.6	.000
	No (309)	28.2	
	DNA (over 65) (5)	20.0	
Former 'restricted category' (more than 5 years for violence, sex or drugs)	Yes (247)	32.0	.426
	No (191)	35.6	
Living arrangements on release	Home (213)	40.4	.000
	Other (90)	35.6	
	Hostel (66)	34.8	
	No fixed accommodation (69)	8.7	
Review number	One (384)	33.1	.838
	Two (51)	37.3	
	Three (3)	33.3	

Appendix 3

Relationship between ROR for a serious offence on parole licence and the parole decision

Actuarial RORS	Number of cases	Number and percentage paroled		Percentage of cases in each risk group
		Number	Percentage	
0%–2%	83	48	57.8	19.0
3%–4%	67	31	46.3	15.3
5%–7%	76	35	46.1	17.4
Total 0%–7% (average 3.5%)	226	114	50.4	51.7
Total 8%–16% (average 10.9%)	124	26	21.0	28.4
17%–25%	45	2	4.5	10.3
26%–39%	25	2	8.0	5.7
40% and higher	17	3	17.6	3.9
Total 17% and higher (average 30%)	87	7	8.0	19.9
Total	437*	147	33.6	100

$\chi2 = 63.0$, 2 df, $p < .000$ *Excludes one case for which data was not available, a foreign national.

Appendix 4

Risk of reconviction form (used for PBIMs, panel members and probation officers)

University of Oxford
Centre for Criminological Research

Research on Discretionary Conditional Release
and Parole Decision-Making

ASSESSMENT OF RISK OF RECONVICTION

Report writer identifier   . . . .

Prisoner number   . . . .

CRO number   . . . .

When answering the following questions, please choose the appropriate band (e.g. very high, moderate etc) and indicate if you can (otherwise use a tick in the box) your estimated percentage (e.g. 33% in the moderate box).

1. WHAT DO YOU ESTIMATE THE RISK TO BE OF THIS PRISONER BEING CONVICTED
OF A **SERIOUS OFFENCE**?
*(This means an offence so serious that it would result in a prison sentence being
imposed)*

DURING THE PERIOD ON **PAROLE** LICENCE **IF** PAROLE WERE GRANTED
*(i.e. between release on **parole** licence and **NPD**)*

	Very High: 80 per cent probability or more
	High: between 60 and 79 per cent
	About 50/50: between 40 and 59 per cent
	Moderate: between 20 and 39 per cent
	Low: between 0 and 19 per cent

WITHIN TWO YEARS FOLLOWING RELEASE FROM PRISON
(whether on parole or at NPD)

i. IF **granted** parole *(i.e. released before **NPD**)*

	Very High: 80 per cent probability or more
	High: between 60 and 79 per cent
	About 50/50: between 40 and 59 per cent
	Moderate: between 20 and 39 per cent
	Low: between 0 and 19 per cent

ii IF **not granted** parole

	Very High: 80 per cent probability or more
	High: between 60 and 79 per cent
	About 50/50: between 40 and 59 per cent
	Moderate: between 20 and 39 per cent
	Low: between 0 and 19 per cent

PLEASE TURN OVER

2. WHAT DO YOU ESTIMATE THE RISK TO BE OF THIS PRISONER BEING CONVICTED OF **ANY OFFENCE**?
(This means any offence which will be recorded in the person's criminal record. It excludes minor motoring offences)

DURING THE PERIOD ON **PAROLE** LICENCE **IF** PAROLE WERE GRANTED
*(i.e. between release on **parole** licence and **NPD**)*

	Very High: 80 per cent probability or more
	High: between 60 and 79 per cent
	About 50/50: between 40 and 59 per cent
	Moderate: between 20 and 39 per cent
	Low: between 0 and 19 per cent

WITHIN TWO YEARS FOLLOWING RELEASE FROM PRISON
(whether on parole or at NPD)

i   IF **granted** parole *(i.e. released before **NPD**)*

	Very High: 80 per cent probability or more
	High: between 60 and 79 per cent
	About 50/50: between 40 and 59 per cent
	Moderate: between 20 and 39 per cent
	Low: between 0 and 19 per cent

ii   IF **not granted** parole

	Very High: 80 per cent probability or more
	High: between 60 and 79 per cent
	About 50/50: between 40 and 59 per cent
	Moderate: between 20 and 39 per cent
	Low: between 0 and 19 per cent

References

Carlisle, Lord (Chairman) (1988) *The Parole System in England and Wales. Report of the Review Committee* (Cm 532). London, HMSO.

Copas, J. B., Marshall, P. and Tarling, R. (1996) *Predicting Reoffending for Discretionary Conditional Release.* Home Office Research Study No. 150. London: Home Office.

Ellis, T. and Marshall, P. (1998) 'Does Parole Work'. *Home Office Research Bulletin 39*, 43-50.

Home Office (1999) *Prison Statistics for England and Wales 1998* (Cm 4430). London: Stationary Office.

H.M. Prison Service (1999) *Parole Newsletter*, No. 4, Spring 1999.

Hood, R. and Shute, S. (1994) *Parole in Transition: Evaluating the Impact and Effects of Changes in the Parole System. Phase One: Establishing the Base-Line.* University of Oxford, Centre for Criminological Research, Occasional Paper No. 13.

Hood, R. and Shute, S. (1995) *Evaluating the Impact and Effects of Changes in the Parole System. Phase Two: Paroling with New Criteria.* University of Oxford, Centre for Criminological Research, Occasional Paper No. 16.

Hood, R. and Shute, S. (1996) 'Parole Criteria, Parole Decisions and the Prison Population: Evaluating the Impact of the Criminal Justice Act 1991'. *Criminal Law Review, 77-87.*

Kershaw, C., Goodman, J. and White, S. (1999) *Reconvictions of offenders sentenced or discharged from prison in 1995, England and Wales.* Home Office Statistical Bulletin, Issue 19/99. London: Home Office.

Lloyd, C., Mair, G. and Hough, M. (1994) *Explaining reconviction rates: a critical analysis.* Home Office Research Study No. 136. London: Home Office.

Maguire, M., Peroud, B. and Raynor, P. (1996) *Automatic Conditional Release: the first two years.* Home Office Research Study No. 156. London: Home Office.

Mannheim, H. and Wilkins, L.T. (1955) *Prediction Methods in Relation to Borstal Training.* London: HMSO.

Monahan, J. and Steadman, H. (1994) 'Towards a Rejuvenation of Risk Assessment' in Monahan, J. and Steadman, H. (eds.), *Violence and Mental Disorder: Developments in Risk Assessment.* Chicago: Chicago University Press.

Nuttall, C. P. *et al.* (1977) *Parole in England and Wales.* Home Office Research Study No. 38. London: HMSO.

Parole Board (1991) *Report of the Parole Board for 1990* (HC 481). London: HMSO.

Parole Board (1994) *Report of the Parole Board for 1993* (HC 450). London: HMSO.

Parole Board (1995) *Report of the Parole Board for 1994* (HC 531). London: HMSO.

Parole Board (1996) *Report of the Parole Board for 1995 and 1995/6* (HC 506). London: The Stationery Office.

Parole Board (1999) *Report of the Parole Board for 1998/99* (HC 809). London: The Stationery Office.

Shepherd, M. (1998) *The Timeliness of Parole Procedures in Establishments.* Adult Males, Parole and Lifer Group, HM Prison Service.

Vennard, J. and Hedderman, C. (1998) 'Effective Interventions with Offenders' in Nuttall C. *et al.* (1998) *Reducing Offending: an assessment of research evidence on ways of dealing with offending behaviour.* Home Office Research Study No. 187. London: Home Office.

Ward, D. (1987) *The Validity of the Reconviction Prediction Score.* Home Office Research Study No. 94. London: Home Office.

West, D. J. (1972) 'Parole in England: an introductory explanation' in West D. J. (ed.), *The Future of Parole.* London: Duckworth.

Publications

List of research publications

The most recent research reports published are listed below. A full list of publications is available on request from the Research, Development and Statistics Directorate, Information and Publications Group.

Home Office Research Studies (HORS)

190. **Trespass and protest: policing under the Criminal Justice and Public Order Act 1994.** Tom Bucke and Zoë James. 1999.

191. **Domestic Violence: Findings from a new British Crime Survey self-completion questionnaire.** Catriona Mirrlees-Black. 1999.

192. **Explaining reconviction following a community sentence: the role of social factors.** Chris May. 1999.

193. **Domestic Violence Matters: an evaluation of a development project.** Liz Kelly. 1999.

194. **Increasing confidence in community sentences: the results of two demonstration projects.** Carol Hedderman, Tom Ellis and Darren Sugg. 1999.

195. **Trends in Crime Revisited.** Simon Field. 1999.

196. **A question of evidence? Investigating and prosecuting rape in the 1990s.** Jessica Harris and Sharon Grace. 1999.

197. **Drug Misuse Declared in 1998: results from the British Crime Survey.** Malcolm Ramsay and Sarah Partridge. 1999.

198. **Modelling and predicting property crime trends in England and Wales.** Sanjay Dhiri, Sam Brand, Richard Harries and Richard Price. 1999.

199. **The right of silence: the impact of the Criminal Justice and Public Order Act 1994.** Tom Bucke, Robert Street and David Brown. 2000.

200. **Attitudes to Crime and Criminal Justice: Findings from the 1998 British Crime Survey.** Joanna Mattinson and Catriona Mirrlees-Black. 2000.

201. **'Tell them so they listen': Messages from young people in custody.** Juliet Lyon, Catherine Dennison and Anita Wilson. 2000.

Research Findings

79.   An evaluation of the prison sex offender treatment programme. Anthony Beech et al. 1998.

80.   Age limits for babies in prison: some lessons from abroad. Diane Caddle. 1998.

81.   Motor projects in England & Wales: an evaluation. Darren Sugg. 1998

82.   HIV/Aids risk behaviour among adult male prisoners. John Strange et al. 1998.

83.   Concern about crime: findings from the 1998 British Crime Survey. Catriona Mirrlees-Black and Jonathan Allen. 1998.

84.   Transfers from prison to hospital - the operation of section 48 of the Mental Health Act 1983. Ronnie Mackay and David Machin. 1998.

85.   Evolving crack cocaine careers. Kevin Brain, Howard Parker and Tim Bottomley. 1998.

86.   Domestic Violence: Findings from the BCS self-completion questionnaire. 1999. Catriona Mirrlees-Black and Carole Byron. 1999.

87.   Incentives and earned privileges for prisoners – an evaluation. Alison Liebling, Grant Muir, Gerry Rose and Anthony Bottoms. 1999.

88.   World Prison Population List. Roy Walmsley. 1999.

89.   Probation employment schemes in inner London and Surrey – an evaluation. Chris Sarno, Michael Hough, Claire Nee and Victoria Herrington. 1999.

90.   Reconviction of offenders sentenced or released from prison in 1994. Chris Kershaw. 1999.

91.   Domestic violence matters: an evaluation of a development project. Liz Kelly. 1999.

92.   Increasing confidence in community sentences. Carol Hedderman, Tom Ellis and Darren Sugg. 1999.

94.   The Prison Population in 1998: a statistical review. Philip White. 1999.

95.   Using Mentors to Change Problem Behaviour in Primary School Children. Ian St James Roberts and Clifford Samial Singh. 1999.

96.   Meeting Need and Challenging Crime in Partnership with Schools. Graham Vulliamy and Rosemary Webb. 1999.

97. **The role of social factors in predicting reconviction for offenders on community penalties.** Chris May. 1999.

98. **Community penalties for fine default and persistent petty offending.** Robin Elliott, Jennifer Airs and Stefan Webb. 1999.

99. **Demanding physical activity programmes for young offenders.** Peter Taylor, Iain Crow, Dominic Irvine and Geoff Nichols. 1999.

100. **The admissibility and sufficiency of evidence in child abuse prosecutions.** Gwynn Davis, Laura Hoyano, Caroline Keenan, Lee Maitland and Rod Morgan. 1999.

101. **Reconviction of offenders sentenced or released from prison in 1995.** Chris Kershaw, Joanne Goodman and Steve White. 1999.

102. **Jury excusal and deferral.** Jennifer Airs and Angela Shaw. 1999.

103. **The cost of Criminal Justice.** Richard Harries. 1999.

104. **Predicting reconvictions for sexual and violent offences using the revised offender group reconviction scale.** Ricky Taylor. 1999.

105. **Making the tag fit: further analysis from the first two years of the trials of curfew orders.** Ed Mortimer, Eulalia and Isabel Walter. 1999.

106. **Drug treatment and testing orders – interim evaluation.** Paul J Turnbull. 1999.

107. **The Victims Charter – an evaluation of pilot projects.** Carolyn Hoyle, Rod Morgan and Andrew Sanders. 1999.

108. **The Milton Keynes Youth Crime Reduction Project.** Alan Mackie and John Burrows. 1999.

109. **The nature and effectiveness of drugs throughcare for released prisoners.** John Burrows, Alan Clarke, Tonia Davison, Roger Tarling and Sarah Webb. 2000

110. **Home detention curfew – the first year of operation.** Kath Dodgson and Ed Mortimer. 2000.

111. **Attitudes to crime and Criminal Justice: Findings from the 1998 British Crime Survey.** Joanna Mattinson and Catriona Mirrlees-Black. 2000.

112. **Problem drug use and probation in London.** Ian Heamden and Alex Harocopos. 2000.

Occasional Papers

Monitoring and evaluation of WOLDS remand prison and comparisons with public-sector prisons, in particular HMP Woodhill. A Keith Bottomley, Adrian James, Emma Clare and Alison Liebling. 1997.

Evaluation of the 'One Stop Shop' and victim statement pilot projects. Carolyn Hoyle, Ed Cape, Rod Morgan and Andrew Sanders. 1998.

Restorative Justice: an overview. Tony Marshall. 1999.

Step 3: an evaluation of the prison sex offender treatment programme. Anthony Beech, Dawn Fisher and Richard Beckett. 1999.

The Impact of the National Lottery on the Horserace Betting Levy: Fourth Report. Sam Brand. 1999.

An assessment of the admissibility and sufficiency of evidence in child abuse prosecutions. Gwynn Davis, Laura Hoyano, Caroline Keenan, Lee Maitland and Rod Morgan. 1999.

Violence at work: findings from the British Crime Survey. Tracey Budd. 1999.

Demanding physical activity programmes for young offenders under probation supervision. Peter Taylor, Iain Crow, Dominic Irvine and Geoff Nichols. 1999.

Youth Justice Pilots Evaluation: Interim report on reparative work and youth offending teams. Jim Dignan. 2000.

New measures for fine defaulters, persistent petty offenders and others: the report of the Crime (Sentences) Act 1997 pilots. Robin Elliott and Jennifer Airs. 2000.

Requests for Publications

Home Office Research Studies, Research Findings and Occasional Papers can be requested from:

Research, Development and Statistics Directorate
Information and Publications Group
Room 201, Home Office
50 Queen Anne's Gate
London SW1H 9AT
Telephone: 020 7273 2084
Facsimile: 020 7222 0211
Internet: http://www.homeoffice.gov.uk/rds/index.htm
E-mail: rds.ho@gtnet.gov.uk